RIGHT RHYTHMIC LIVING

A Path to Healing

9-ETHE

RIGHT RHYTHMIC LIVING

A Path to Healing

Claire Etheridge, Ph.D.

To order additional copies of this book, contact:
Xlibris Corporation
1-888-7-XLIBRIS
www.Xlibris.com
Orders@Xlibris.com

Contents

PART I
Physical Healing

PART II
Healing Our Woundedness

PART III
Spiritual Discipline

Summary

The purpose of the book is to help others. It is as if she is saying, "Here I am; this is what happened to me; this is what I learned from the experiences in my life; maybe you can benefit by my sharing it with you." Very simple, very humble, very honest. It is clear that strength through adversity was modeled to her.

Helen and John Watkins, Ph.D.
University of Montana

Claire E. Etheridge, Ph.D.

Biography

Dr. Etheridge has taught at several colleges and universities, the last being the University of California at Irvine as a medical psychologist. She is well known for her workshops sponsored by the Institute for Advanced Studies, which she founded. She authored *Headstart in Action* during the 1960's, translated into Spanish and Portuguese for South American readers. She developed a psychological screening test for pre-school children.

With her spiritual director, Reverend Robert Cornelison, she founded a non-profit religious organization, An Order of Healers: A Monastery without Walls, and serves as Abbas, giving workshops, retreats and spiritual direction.

She has two grown children, reads science fiction and goes to the wilderness for renewal. And she is still asking questions.

*To my family, who have
supported me, educated me, disciplined me,
and loved me through my journey.*

Acknowledgments

Elizabeth Edgington, who proofread and provided input for the first draft of the manuscript and encouraged me through several more drafts; Paul Turpin, for writing the **PREFACE**; my daughter, Rene' Riley, who proofed and inputted the final draft, and for her encouragement; Leon Bolen, for his invaluable assistance in bringing the manuscript to book form; my sister, Elaine Deatherage, for her insights on music in the chapter "This is my song;" Joan Ririe, for her perennial ability to see an "up" side to seeming calamities; Dr. E.V. Pullias, former Dean of Pepperdine College, who taught me wisdom; the Rev. Robert Cornelison, my Spiritual Director, who taught and modeled the Creator's unconditional love for us all; Janet Mentgen, for teaching healing from the concept of "energy medicine;" Carolyn Yap, M.D., who shared generously of her vast knowledge of nutrition and the importance of love to the people we helped; Madeleine L'Engle, for her writer's workshops and inspirational books; Mary Betty Fisher, who gave me my first copy of *Letters of the Scattered Brotherhood*; Fanny Crosby, who wrote the words to many hymns that touch my heart; Helen and John Watkins, Ph.D., my professional mentors, for their teachings and encouragement; my music consultant, Jack Moe, a retired classical musician; Donald Schafer, M.D., for his detailed and always helpful critical reviews; my parents and extended family who taught me to question; and especially those clients and patients who shared their stories with me. For without their trust, this book would not have been written.

Forward

Donald W. Schafer, M.D.
Professor Emeritus, University of California at Irvine

When I received Claire Etheridge's book and noted especially the sub-title—*A Path to Healing*—I read it with intense interest. I have known Claire since 1970, shortly after we both joined the staff of the Department of Psychiatry and Human Behavior at the University of California Irvine, California College of Medicine. Therefore, I recognized that some aspects of the book are autobiographical; and how appropriate that is. When a book of this nature is written, it is usually obvious that it is meant to be a monument to one's self, at least unconsciously. However this is not such a book. Because she lives what she writes, she is completely under her own control; what she writes is about herself, her faith and especially about her relationships with others. She *knows* that her healing of others as well as of herself is possible only through the inner faith that makes life so meaningful. And she writes about this beautifully.

The strength that she, herself, developed over the years should be shared. Using that strength and faith to help people is what makes this book so warm and full of wisdom. She does not advocate the substitution of her messages and instructions for the treatments involved in conventional medicine. She does not tell you to get rid of your physicians, nurses and hospitals. You must augment the best that is available as provided by those personages, and then follow the path of healing as she advocates. Naturally, you should modify your own path for your own needs and abilities.

In other words, following this path to healing by developing

Right Rhythmic Living will produce "cures" that will amaze others, especially the physicians. I started to say that even if it doesn't work, you will live a better life. *But this is wrong.* It does work. Not only to a better life, but to better health. As a physician, I know that the Autonomic Nervous System is close enough to the surface to be influenced by both our inner and outer worlds. So is the Immune System. Here is the path for those of you who really wish to be healthy in both body and mind.

Endorsements

"Having known Dr. Etheridge for almost 30 years, I know that she walks what she talks. We're fortunate to have her share with us her journey to health and wholeness." —*Robert L. Cornelison, M.Div., retired Episcopal priest, Los Angeles Diocese.*

"This simple story has mysteriously wound its way through my life, planting the seeds of change." —*Brenda Anderson, nurse healer, Smithers, Canada.*

"The wonderful book, *Right Rhythmic Living*, has taught me and encouraged me to live a life dedicated to doing God's work. The lessons of holy silence, holy leisure, right relationships—and how to care for my physical, emotional, and mental bodies—have guided me through the process of daily life. This is life-changing reading. —*Janet Mentgen, BSN; founder, Healing Touch International, Lakewood, Colorado.*

"This book has made significant contributions to both my personal and professional life." —*Carolyn Roth, Major Gifts Officer, California Nature Conservancy, Sacramento, Davis, California.*

Right Rhythmic Living is based on solid psychological principles." —*Eirene Wong-Liang, Ph.D., clinical psychologist, Houston, Texas.*

"My, what a lovely book—warm, soft, sincere, spiritual, and yet there underlies a strength that anyone might envy. We both read it, and it contained so much wisdom—wisdom that hopefully the reader will use. It is quite an autobiography. You sprinkle details of your life, but not too much. Too much would overwhelm the purpose of the book, which is to help others. It's as if you are saying, 'Here I am; this is what happened to me; this is what I learned from the experiences in my life; maybe you can benefit by my sharing it with you.' Very simple, very humble, very honest. We were particularly interested in your early life, about which we knew very little. It is clear that strength through adversity was modeled to you. And we can hear the sound of your laughter through your description of those early years." *—Helen and John Watkins, Ph.D., Professor emeritus, University of Montana.*

Preface

The aim of this book is to outline a path for people to become healers—healers both of themselves and of others. To heal another, you must first be able to heal yourself. How can healing be accomplished? The most powerful force of healing is love. Love exists only in the flow of relationships, because love needs an object. Relationships that allow us to heal are those that are with others, the earth, the cosmos, and God.

The most encompassing love of all is spiritual (*agape*) love, for it includes all the cosmos and casts out none. Spiritual love of all is a constant goal. A divine example of spiritual love is Christ's suffering so that God could heal all mankind.

Healing is the relief of pain and the renewal of life through a regeneration of the spirit. It is less an action performed than a process given an opportunity to happen. Above all, healing is a natural outcome of love. In our modern lives we have too many things that we try to make happen by force. Healing is not possible this way; it is the result of a relaxation, an unclenching of tension, a release from fear that is made visible to us when we cease to flinch (inwardly or outwardly) at every tiny intrusion. And, because healing is about real human beings, it is a constant process; it does not just happen once and for all.

Healing is not an easy concept for modern people; we tend to think of healing in medical terms. Consider the difference between curing and healing: The thrust of modern (*allopathic*) medicine is to cure; in pre-modern days, the essence of healing was to help the person heal her- or himself.

The difference between curing and healing involves fundamentally different orientations as to the place of the person in the world, and the very nature of the world itself. Modern medicine's acme of success lies in what it can cure, such as the elimination of the bacterial plagues of earlier centuries, and biomechanical solutions to organic problems through modern surgical techniques and technology.

Outside of its areas of strength, though, allopathic medicine is reticent, if not entirely silent, on how we can deal with difficulties for which it has no answers. We are always left with the conundrum that medicine cannot cure death, and with the implication that the inevitability of death is somehow a judgment on medicine's success or lack of it.

Traditional medicine has always distinguished between illness and the end of life. I believe the first is worth every effort to ameliorate, and the second is to be respected as the culmination of life and, in the wisdom of most cultures, the beginning of another, entirely spiritual, aspect of being. The first step in the process of treating the problem of pain is one that requires healing at every level of our being.

Prologue

"I got rhythm, I got rhythm, I got rhythm, who could ask for anything more?"
—Ira Gershwin

Rhythm. We all "feel better" after a good night's sleep.

Rhythm. We feel invigorated after a walk in nature, especially at dawn or dusk.

Rhythm. The harmony of a Schubert symphony or an Ella Fitzgerald ballad.

The title of this book, *Right Rhythmic Living*, assumes rhythm is a given in our lives. And that "Right Rhythmic Living" leads to healing and health. "Right" means that we are in touch with our own rhythms and those of the natural world. Right Rhythmic Living means we are living our lives in harmony with those rhythms as a way of life. Our model for right rhythm comes from the earth itself, with its cycles and seasons. As the song from "Fiddler on the Roof goes:

> "Sunrise, sunset, sunrise, sunset, quickly flow the
> years. One season following another, laden with
> happiness and tears."

The beginnings and endings of our lives and *relationships* are a natural phenomena within the rhythms of our "life's story."
In disease, or dis-ease, we have "lost our rhythm," not only indi-

vidually but in relationship with one another, the earth, the cosmos, and God. It is only by regaining our right rhythm—in ourselves, as well in community with others—that we find health and peace of mind.

As we lose touch with ourselves we lose our natural healthy rhythm. Sometimes a culture or place is so out of balance with its natural rhythm that pain is suffered by all. The earth may be poisoned, or the government may be totalitarian. Hopefully, the pain we feel as individuals leads us to do our part to correct what is out of balance, out of harmony, and out of rhythm without doing harm in the process. No matter how out of balance we may feel, a good place to begin is to tell our story. I believe that understanding where we come from and what influences have shaped our lives is a prerequisite to becoming a teacher and a healer.

I am fortunate to come from a storytelling family. We were encouraged to talk about our day, and if we were still puzzled or in a quandary, instead of providing pat answers, my Daddy would say, "Just study on it." So I learned to go deep inside myself and listen within.

In this way, I learned that: (1) I probably knew a lot more than I gave myself credit for, based on life experiences, and (2) it was important to value my own opinions, life experiences and sense of personal integrity.

As the years went by, I began to reflect on my early memories, to distill what I learned, and to share it with others.

In this book I share my story and hopefully inspire you to find your own.

> "THIS IS MY STORY,
> THIS IS MY SONG. . . ."
> —Fanny Crosby

I was born in a small frame house in Kilgore, Texas, in the depths of the Great Depression, 1931. My proud farmer father had gone to Texas from Oklahoma seeking work. My birth was difficult for my mother, as she was sick, lonely, and unhappy in Texas. We moved back to dust bowl Oklahoma and in with my mother's family as soon as she was able to travel. I was about six weeks old. Living in the large house at 10 West Ridgewood in Shawnee, Oklahoma were my mother and father, my grandparents, five aunts, and two uncles. I was the only grandchild for the first four years of my life, and was treasured and protected in that family group even after we moved into our own home just before my second birthday. The love and cosseting I received gave me the confidence to reach out for help and expect it to be forthcoming through a subsequent lifetime of joy and pain.

My maternal grandfather, a general contractor, was a benevolent dictator. The story is told that when we first came to live in his home he danced around with me in his arms and declared, "Whoever harms a hair of this baby's head will answer to me." Grandpa Jimmie was a little like God to me. He knew right from wrong. He told people what to do. And he provided for us all until the Great Depression took all he had in the mid-thirties. Unable to support his family, he left in search of work and was not heard from for two years. We always honored and respected him, even in his illness when he returned, a broken, yet proud man.

Although quieter, my father was equally protective, and it became natural for me to expect all men to be my protectors, and "unnatural" when they were not. Later on, as an adolescent, it was natural and easy for me to call God, "Father."

My father's grandfather was a doctor in the wilderness of Arkansas during the Civil War. When he was kidnapped and killed by bushwhackers, his pregnant wife became the folk doctor for an area that was later known as Sulfur Rock, Arkansas. Though pregnant, she continued to make rounds in a horse and buggy, taking care of the sick, as she was the closest thing they had to a doctor.

When my great-grandmother gave birth to my grandmother she was attended by five neighbors whom she had trained to be midwives. The baby, her youngest, my father's mother, was named Mary Ellen.

Little Mary Ellen accompanied her mother on her rounds and absorbed "doctoring" with her mother's milk. Married at 16, she lost her last three children before they were five, but raised eight boys and two girls, all of whom lived to a ripe old age. The youngest to survive was my father, Joseph Marion, born October 13,1899. Mary Ellen tended her family with the folk knowledge of her mother and her husband's medical training, and thus continued the family tradition of farmin' and "doctorin.'" The man she married was deafened by a close lightning strike, so she became his interface to the outside world, continuing the matriarchal tradition of her own mother.

As the youngest, my father lived at home with his mother and cared for her until he married two weeks shy of his thirtieth birthday, October 1, 1930. Raised by a strong pioneer woman used to hard work, and with family ties as strong as survival itself, his view on women was as helpmate, friend and lover, in that order. You did not just marry another person; you married into a family, into a social support network. As he raised me, those values became my values, my rule of life.

Before he died, my father told me of his gradual growing awareness of the sacredness of life. Once, when we were camping in Yosemite, we went out to chop wood for our campfire.

"You know," he said, "when I was a kid I'd think nothing of shooting a squirrel or a rabbit just because it was there. But I've changed. Who is that man that went to Africa and helped people? Saw a special on him the other night on television."

"Albert Schweitzer, Daddy?"

"Yes, I think that was his name. Reverence for life. He's right. Always remember that." Long pause. "I wish I'd learned that sooner."

My dad's family were pioneers on both sides. The Deatherage side pushed west from our Virginia Plantation in the 1700's. We survived by observing and respecting the "signs" of nature, the seasons, the animals, the earth, the crops, and people's behavior. We took our basically English culture with us. Our sense of honor, integrity, respect for the land, duty to God and family. Our values were fair play, protection of women and children, and cooperation for the good of all. We learned to get along with the native Americans, to respect the five civilized tribes (my great-grandfather married into the Cherokee nation) to abhor the white men who broke their treaties, and to find God in nature, in the stars, in the budding of spring, and in the cry of a newborn baby.

We learned to think things out, to "study on it," to observe the world of people, animals, and growing things. When I was one year old, we moved from my grandfather's house and spent the next seven years on a dirt farm and oil field in Potawattamie county, Oklahoma. Although there were no neighbors within a mile or so, dozens of relatives were within 25 miles to visit and render help. Thus, I was raised with the unique regard for family, God, nature, and healing that can only be known by those who derived a living from the land before mechanized farming became the norm.

My mother was a schoolteacher and had been raised in the small town of Tecumseh, Oklahoma (population 2,000). She found life during the depression difficult, and frequent visits to her family were occasions of joy and relief. Supported by family on both sides, we had little time or desire for any social life other than church suppers, potlucks, and visits from the Agricultural Agent.

My mother was born February 8, 1905, near Tecumseh in what was then Indian Territory. Her father, Jimmie, was the youngest son in his large family in Missouri and had left home for the Oklahoma Land Rush of 1889. Teddy Roosevelt was President and "rugged individualism" was the national credo.

Her family came to the United States from England and Ireland. (Up until her death at age 91, my mother had a peaches-and-cream complexion. Ireland was always her favorite country. It was never conquered by the Romans and my mother was never conquered by anybody.)

She once came for a conference where I delivered a paper. It was in San Francisco at a Japanese hotel and Ernst Freud, Sigmund's nephew and only surviving relative, sat with us at dinner. Although quite frail, he and my mother had a very spirited conversation. She told him he should eat more so he wouldn't "dry up and blow away." He meekly (or politely) agreed.

As I said, her father, Grandpa Jimmie, ruled the roost and her mother Clara Ader (also one-quarter Cherokee) had an active life raising babies (with my mother's help), gardening, cooking, quilting, and singing, the latter especially in the local Cumberland Presbyterian Church (of conservative Scottish origin).

Her mother was Clara Ader Jones (Welsh), daughter of Daime Adline (native American) and John Walton Edmondson (English). Her father, James Washington Richardson (English) was the youngest of Mary Anne Foss (Taylor) and James William Richardson. Her ancestors settled in Kentucky and pushed to Illinois and Missouri.

My mother's favorite story is about my father's mother, Mary Ellen (Granny to me), and her older sister. During the Civil War Confederate soldiers took their cows. Her 12-year-old sister followed the soldiers to their camp and demanded the return of the cows. And got them back! Talk about raw courage—the women in our family have it in spades.

After my mother graduated from East Central State Teacher's College in Ada, Oklahoma, and received a lifetime teacher's credential, she decided she wanted to go teach in Alaska. Alaska! She was 19 years old and Papa Jimmie put his foot down. No way.

My mother held resolute, however, and my sisters took her to Alaska for the first time when she was 81, and again when she was 86. "It's so beautiful," she'd say, eyes glistening. She even went on a helicopter ride to see the glaciers and chartered a boat to Bird Island in rough weather. No stopping *my* mother—arbiter of morals, mother to all, who knew no Master but her God.

From those humble beginnings it is no wonder I experienced another culture shock when I went to college. I began college at what was then called Sacramento Junior College. I had a hard time with academia. I did not fit in. I just did not think in the way they did or find valuable its stated goals.

When I took my first psychology course as a freshman in college in 1949, I was told that psychology was the science of the psyche, which meant mind. (I have since learned psyche's root meaning is "soul.") Then I proceeded to learn that the objective of psychology was to predict and control behavior! Shades of Orwell's *1984*. Astute observer and straight shooter my family heritage had taught me to be, I went from an A to a B in more than one class when I questioned the premises on which the teachers based their conclusions.

It took me a while to figure out that these premises were sacred cows. And that the kind of cow would vary from class to class, teacher to teacher, and school to school. I learned the hard way, by asking embarrassing questions:

Q: "What makes something a science?"

A: "When it can be measured objectively."

Naive in my assumption that we were seeking truth, I continued: "Why do you say psychology is a science when it can not be measured? If our behavior is dependent on the unconscious mind to a great degree, and if, by definition, the unconscious mind is unconscious, how can we study it?"

And to another teacher who didn't believe in the unconscious, "If there is no unconscious mind, how do we explain doodles? Everybody doodles." To which this teacher sternly replied, "I don't." I decided to drop the question, and she decided to drop my grade.

And again, "If we study the mind by observing behavior only, and a person has socially acceptable behavior until one fateful day when he kills himself, beats his wife, embezzles funds, etc., how do we account for the precursors of that behavior? If you say the person had behaviors that we just did not notice, how can you prove it? And why is this conclusion, based on your guess or assumption, any more valid than mine?" That did it. I wasn't called on to ask anymore questions in *that* class. Grade? C. Even though all my exams received A's.

Later I started reading psychological "studies" and it seemed to me that my father had more common sense in his big toe than the learned "researchers" had in their brains. Skinner was in vogue and children were to be "conditioned" like rats. *Rats?* What about souls, and human dignity and love and freedom?!

The one assumption they made that really made me angry (mostly because I could not break through their so-called logic) ran like this: Mind is a product of brain function, therefore degree of intelligence is dependent upon the size of the brain. Said brain resided in skull, therefore the larger the skull, the larger the brain, and the more intelligent the species. Therefore, men are "smarter" than women and adults are more intelligent than children.

Wait a minute! Up shot my hand. "Then why have I always been considered the smartest in my class if my head is so small I have to wear a child's size hat?" I was told I just had no grasp of mental functioning.

Somehow with the help of choir, drama, history of the theater, and oral interpretation, I weathered my first two years of college with a grade point average sufficient for a scholarship to Pepperdine College, a church of Christ school in Los Angeles (now Pepperdine University in Malibu). There we finally began to discuss *emotion*, and real *feelings*. We began to learn that feelings are related to behavior.

But the books and the teachers still talked about the mind—mental processes and emotions as if they were synonymous. Which I *knew* they were not. Although we paid lip service to emotion, all scientific writing had to be in the objective voice, to never say "I", "we", or admit to a feeling. Fortunately I was allowed to express my true feelings verbally and stated that these premises were pretty dumb.

Later on in graduate school at Florida State University I wrote a paper on the psychophysiology of emotion, and studied the great neurological thinkers of that time, receiving my Ph.D. in 1963. Here I found that the sacred cows of most undergraduate teachers and texts were based on their personal ideas about the mind and emotions, which did not correlate with neurobiology. There was no coherent body of knowledge to prove anyone's pet assumptions. There were theories based on an inadequate base of scientific observation and measurement. And as time has gone on, most of these theories have changed.

Science was such a puzzle. As the song, "Over the Rainbow" says: "Who can explain it? Who can tell us why?"

We all grow up with contradictions, from our parents, from our culture, from our education, with the changing world view.

At Pepperdine College I was most fortunate to have a master teacher to give me principles by which I could begin to resolve the various paradoxes that I experienced. I credit Dr. E. V. Pullias with the wisdom he taught me to help me as life became more complicated, contradictory, and painful. One maxim: "Integrate at a higher level." This advice is what I followed in graduate school to resolve the paradox of science, emotion, and "sacred cow." Another maxim: "Ultimately there is only a spiritual solution, but we may spend a lifetime finding it." I am grateful to all my teachers, but especially to Dr. Pullias.

PART I

Physical Healing

Chapter 1

Physical Clearing

Just as the journey of a thousand miles begins with a first step, so too our resolutions to effect changes in our lives begin with physical changes, small at first, which we can control. Each day's activities need to become part of a new habit of life, and habits require some conscious care and feeding before they become naturally intuitive for us: self care of the body, attunement of the spirit, and physical care of the material logistics of our lives. We all eat, sleep and clothe ourselves. These functions require preparation. We enter into the rhythm of life as we participate fully in the routine of physical work around the maintenance of self and home each day.

The goal is to allow our rhythms to flow naturally from one another in the present moment; working, relaxing, socializing, singing, creating, meditating, dancing, exercising, reading, and sleeping deeply. By cultivating physical conditions in our lives that nurture rather than stress us, we can regain our equilibrium.

We always need to recover our equilibrium because we lose it in the course of living, myself included. In spite of my childhood promise to myself to always tell the truth, as I became subject to the pressures of adolescent society and the young adult's need to conform, I lost my early sense of self-trust. I lost my confidence, my health, and also lost touch with the rhythms of life. Although I never lost my moorings of belief in a God of love and of living by the Golden Rule of doing unto others as I would have them do unto me, I abused my physical body through ignorance and neglect.

Abruptly dislocated from an Oklahoma farm to California suburbs at age nine, I felt like a displaced person. In order to adapt socially, I abandoned some of the healthy ways that seemed to be naturally a part of country living. Later in my life, after a health and domestic crisis in my thirties led to a breakdown of my endocrine system and a breakup of my marriage, I moved my children to the beach, and we slowly began to rebuild. The accumulation of a lifetime's stresses brought home to me the insidious toll we pay.

Thankfully, good fortune provides teachers along the way. May we all be alert to the teachers in our lives to help us along the journey. May we learn to listen as they gently lead us back to differentiating our inner truth from our acquired social adaptation—or maladaptation, as is often the case. For that is what Right Rhythmic Living is: learning or relearning the truth about ourselves—our bodies, our emotions, our social selves—and then heeding, believing and healing from the truth that comes from within rather than from maladaptive social conformities.

My teachers enabled me to deal with the pain in my own life. It was only because I had gone through my own physical clearing and search for healing that I was able, in my psychotherapy practice, to resonate to my patients' cries for help and to provide information and encouragement for them to participate meaningfully in their own healing process. Understanding the natural rhythms of life creates a necessary foundation on which to build.

Common Problems

Years ago, before the term was fashionable, I began to be aware that about half of the people who came to my office with emotional difficulties were really suffering from stress. Depression, anxiety, panic attacks, and many family conflicts had their roots in unhealthy living habits that culminated in distress. Over time I put together a Life Style Inventory that pinpointed the disorder and pointed me in the direction of the areas that were out of balance.

The complaint of depression was a good example. What came up over and over again was poor diet, little or no exercise, and inadequate sleep. (Typical symptoms of depression are poor appetite and early-morning awakening.)

It amazes patients that I assess their fluid intake. "How much water do you drink? Juice? Milk? Alcoholic beverages? Soft drinks?" I have found most people thrive best by eliminating all beverages in between meals but pure water, suggesting that they even carry water with them and drink a glass of water every hour. I carry water in my car and order water with lemon at restaurants.

Then I assess the patient's diet by asking what they usually eat. I emphasize fresh food, fruits and vegetables, fresh meats, uncooked nuts and seeds. Food that is lately exposed to the sun and the earth, not processed foods or food laced with sugar. By adding a complete B-vitamin supplement during the recovery period, and fiber for elimination, I usually notice the person begins to perk up after the first week!

This particular regime alone has been known to ameliorate symptoms of depression, obesity, constipation, premenstrual tension and chronic anxiety. In learning to heal ourselves and others, we need to take a closer look at the total physical lifestyle of a person to reestablish routines in a rhythm of life.

Often times, as my patients would begin to "clean up their act," so to speak, they would also begin to take better care of themselves physically.

One lady—and I have had this same scenario repeated literally hundreds of times—who was exhausted, depressed, drinking too much coffee, eating too much "junk food" as she called it; complained of feeling tired "all the time." I suggested she might like to go to bed earlier and gradually decrease her caffeine intake. After two months of going to bed as soon as it was dark, she started perking up and said that the best thing that ever happened to her was my giving her permission to rest.

One high-powered salesman for a large corporation announced to me he had been studying the comparative health of those who ate red meat and those who did not, and decided quite on his own that as part of his weight reduction regime, he would change to a high-fiber, low-animal-protein diet. Only after he became *aware* and committed to his own well-being was he ready to take better care of his physical body.

Another place to start in our assessment of ourselves is with the physical body. What hurts? What is broken or bruised or strained? Whatever it is, it is not broken like a car; we cannot simply replace the damaged parts. It is more like treating the "failure to thrive" syndrome in children; we need to respond to an out-of-rhythm (dysrhythmic) life style.

When my children were little, I taught them a nursery song about how carrots grow:
"You water it
You pull the weeds
Carrots grow from carrot seeds"
For me as an adult, this means establishing a Right Rhythmic Living pattern, providing what I need and deleting those things that debilitate my growth or health.

Of all the first steps that one could take in setting about taking control over one's physical life, I found that one of the best places to start is with breathing.

Breathing

Breathing is the one physiological function that responds easily to both the voluntary and involuntary nervous systems, which makes it an excellent candidate for a first step. I can think "breathe deeply" and do so; or I can not give my breathing a thought in the world and my body automatically begins to breathe by itself. When we force ourselves to breathe unclean air and to adapt to tense situations, the rhythm of our breathing is disrupted. By contrast, I found that slow deep breathing not only facilitated going into an *alpha state* (a brainwave pattern elicited by meditation or prayer) that quieted pain, but also helped me begin to establish other right rhythms in my life.

Rhythmic breathing is a precursor to good health, both physical and emotional. Deep breathing massages all the organs in the trunk and abdomen, increasing blood circulation and optimal functioning. Sometimes we are so out of touch with our breathing habits we need a friend (or someone we spend much time with throughout the day) to monitor our breathing and help us become aware of our breathing habits: How do we hold our shoulders? Tight, elevated shoulders, even slightly so, hinder correct breathing and thereby restrict the constant message the breathing muscles give to the abdominal organs, clearing them and contributing to their good circulation. I get tight shoulders when I am worried. I found that when I breathe deeply, my posture shifts a little bit, realigning my entire muscular/skeletal system to the gravitational pull of the earth. I like to think that realignment is an indication of restoring a natural resonance.

Impediments to life show up in how we breathe, and these bad habits of breathing often show up in physical symptoms. I used to get tension headaches. I was a shallow chest breather. It was how I held my shoulders—as if I started to shrug them, then kept them a little bit high as if to protect myself from being hit. Constantly tensed shoulder and neck muscles are common; it is the beginning of a flinch, which we all unfortunately learn as children; in my case, I was socially hit by ridicule from other children.

Changing my breathing habits was difficult to do by the time I reached my thirties. Finally, I learned the pillow technique:

Sit down on the floor with a blanket and three pillows. Put one little pillow under your head, a bigger one under your knees and the biggest one on your tummy. As you inhale, watch the pillow on your tummy. As you inhale, the pillow should rise; as you exhale, the pillow should fall. Place one hand on your chest and one hand under the pillow on your tummy. The chest hand should be relatively still. The belly hand should rise and fall rhythmically with an unmeasured pause at the end of the exhale. Once you are rising and falling in the appropriate places of your anatomy, slow your breathing. Try counting slowly to seven as you inhale (about one per second) and to eight as you exhale (to allow for the pause at the end of the exhale).

Wow, this was very difficult for an anxiety-ridden single parent trying to create a new life in a new community. I was told to breathe for five minutes in this position before I got out of bed in the morning and before I went to sleep at night. I started falling asleep more easily after the first week. Then I added five minutes of "floor" breathing when I wanted to decompress after work or before I had to make an important decision.

After a couple of weeks I had the rhythm down pat and began to breathe correctly other times as well. The rhythm of our breathing can be used as a paradigm for the rhythm of our life:

Take it in,

Let it go,

Rest.

Vigorous at times, slow and easy at others: an activity that is both conscious and unconscious.

The physical body gives us feedback to help us understand what Right Rhythmic Living is. But first I have to tune in; I have to be aware of what I am feeling before I can tell what it means.

When I have worked long enough, my muscles want to rest. When I have been in one position too long, they want me to stretch. When I am bursting with energy, my flower beds call me to be weeded. When fever lays me low, I do not want to get out of bed.

How many times have we allowed our conscious selves to be distracted and ignore the feelings of our bodies? I have to listen to what my body is telling me. And I have to trust that it is right; that doing what my physical self needs is the healthiest, most healing way to live.

Sleep

As useful as tools may be, I sometimes rue the day that electric lights and alarm clocks supplanted our biological time clocks of sleep and wakefulness.

To get back into a natural rhythm, I devised the following discipline for myself. At dusk, I do not turn on the lights, or the radio or the television or anything electrical. Instead I shall light a candle or a fire in the fireplace. I do not look at the clock. I pretend I am in a dress rehearsal for an earthquake. (I live in California. For you, it may be a tornado, hurricane, snowstorm, or flood.) When I get sleepy, I go to bed. Inevitably I go right to sleep. When I wake up, if it is daylight, I get up and begin my daily routine. If it is still dark, and not time to get up, I meditate until I go back to sleep.

At first when I started this routine, I was surprised how tired I was, how attuned I was to noise and how quiet I became inside. By permitting sleep to be a natural rhythmic cycle instead of a forced one, work became simply part of a daily routine.

Establishing a rhythmic daily routine is a little like making bread. I think of the wet ingredients as all the active things I do, and the dry ingredients as all the passive things I do. Sleep is like baking—do not disturb until done. And just as it does not make any difference which ingredient I put in the blender first, it does not make any difference whether I meditate and pray, shower or walk first. But they must all be included and mixed together. Rhythmically. Active and passive.

As I was learning to get back in rhythm with myself, my physical being, my biological time clock, it helped me to do many household routines that I had given up. When I began to simplify my life, I let my household helpers move on to others. With an every-other-week cleaning service for heavy jobs, I began to do my own laundry again, arrange my own flowers, clean up my own kitchen, and water my own plants. As I did, I became more grounded and more aware of the cycles of maintenance for my house and myself.

I allowed time to take care of the material things I had surrounded myself with—and discovered there were too many of them! I learned that I needed to simplify my material possessions, a lesson that would have remained unlearned if I had paid helpers.

The emphasis is on becoming conscious of what is necessary to maintain our lives, so that we eliminate what is unnecessary, and only give time and energy to those things that contribute to our lives.

Body Movement

In developing a treatment program, I quickly originated a walking program of 20 minutes a day, building up to two hours a day, allowing for individual differences and preferences.

Exercise has to be developed individually for each person and should involve:

1. Contact the earth through walking on it,
2. Aerobic enough to help the heartbeat accelerate, then rapidly return to normal.
3. Something you like and will do on a daily basis.

Actually a good brisk walk can usually fulfill all of these requirements. So will playing tennis on a clay court. Or a walk, a swim and lifting a few weights, even as little as eight ounces.

Physical work is akin to exercise. Akin, but not identical—the main difference is that physical work often just involves muscle constriction without the corresponding relaxation. For example, doing biceps curls with weights involves letting the arm straighten completely in relaxation on a one-to-one basis with the constriction that bends the arm and lifts the weight. The similar constricting motion of a plumber working with pipe is only irregularly relieved.

Exercise is for the specific purpose of building and strengthening the physical body, a noble purpose. Physical work is to accomplish a goal; exercise is the beneficial side effect that comes with the satisfaction of accomplishment. I was taught by my agrarian parents that physical work is an honorable virtue. This morning I steamed rice, baked corn bread and put black beans in the oven. Then I mopped the kitchen floor on my hands and knees. Not only did I do the necessary stretching and weight lifting, I began the day with quite a sense of accomplishment before I turned to this writing, whose rewards are less definite. I know I will get a clean floor; the words I write may end up in the wastebasket.

I do not believe our agrarian ancestors had to worry about exercise. They walked everywhere they went, they lifted heavy weights in carrying out the normal chores of house and field, and they danced in celebration for hours on end. My father square-danced Saturday night *after* a day's work on the farm!

I do not advocate doing laundry on rocks in the River Ganges, but I do suggest we spend some time every day using our physical bodies to take care of our living space and cultivate our gardens— *water and pull the weeds.*

Gardening is an excellent way to get exercise and commune with nature at the same time; many healers I have studied worked in their gardens with pleasure and pride. Agnes Sanford, who wrote *The Healing Light,* scolded the vestry of her husband's church for taking her flower garden and paving it over for parking! Olga Worall, author of *The Gift of Healing,* took pleasure not only in growing plants but accelerating their health and growth through the laying on of hands and prayer.

After knee surgery 20 years ago, I had to start from scratch, so to speak, with learning to walk again. I needed the services of a skilled physical therapist for six months to note my progress and tell me how much of what to do next.

After my back injury later in life, I found I did not know how to begin to build up my muscles without hurting myself. Even selecting the 11-ounce can of asparagus over the eight-ounce can of tomato sauce caused unnecessary stress, pain and delay. I was mortified at lifting only eight ounces until I discovered another person who began with two.

Physical therapists, exercise coaches, body builders, yoga teachers and tennis coaches all have their place in helping build strong muscular bodies, as do gardeners, housekeepers and farmers.

The Earth

I learned about the healing energies of the earth from Olga Worall, a healer in the Methodist church who was studied at Duke, UCLA, and the University of London. She taught me that, depending on where you live and work, the energy from the earth is ours for the taking. Free of charge. Just by taking off our shoes and walking on the earth. If asphalt is everywhere, she suggested we try the track at the local high school, a park, or the beach and wear shoes only if we have to. Patios can be created with rocks, plants and streams, not just to look good but to experience. She taught us to lay board-walks directly over dirt to allow earth energy to come through, and that we can walk on gravel (composed of small rocks), tile or brick. "Walk every day," she admonished. "Get grounded." Only when the healer is grounded to the earth does the energy flow, and circulate freely.

For health there must be a flow from our feet to the tops of our heads, a continuous free-flowing feedback loop. As a healer can not give what she does not have, it behooves us to walk daily on the earth as much as possible.

The Sun

As we get in touch with our own biological rhythms, we find ourselves sleeping and waking with the sun. Getting in touch with the right rhythm of light and dark.

When I was in Badgestein, Austria, one October, there was a large building with a domed glass roof with rows of chairs; it wasn't some sort of auditorium, it was a solarium where people came just to sit in the sun and soak up the rays regardless of the weather.

People in northern regions are more aware of their need for sun than those in southern ones, because they often become depressed through lack of sunlight in winter. Science's discovery of sunlight's role in vitamin D formation and other physiological benefits only confirms the folk wisdom my mother knew: "Why she just isn't getting enough sunlight. Open the drapes, put her in the sun." English nannies religiously take their charges to the park "for the sun."

Here's an excellent way for office workers to recharge themselves in the middle of the day: instead of sitting in a restaurant or at your desk, take some healthful food to a park where you can absorb the nourishment of the earth and sun as well as your food.

I have come to believe that a healer needs one to two hours of sun (indirect, please) and one to two hours on the earth every day. What a wonderful reason to tend my garden! For the energies the healer are to work with are so powerful that we must have a strong body to contain them.

Jesus taught in the parable of the wineskins:

> "Neither is new wine put into old wineskins; if it is, the
> skins burst, and the wine is spilled, and the skins are
> destroyed; but new wine is put into fresh wineskins, and
> so both are preserved."
>
> —Matthew 9:17

Just as we cannot put new wine in old skins, we cannot put new energies in underdeveloped bodies.

Nutrition

As a budding psychologist, I was first taught in treating eating disorders that "food is mother"; by working out the relationship with the mother, the eating problem would subside. Oh my! Or, as the Cole Porter song says, "It ain't necessarily so." It is much more complicated! What about the obese person who was molested as a child, and later built up the fat as body armor? What about food intolerances and allergies?

Research in recent years suggests that we might not be as well nourished as we think we are, despite our country's wealth of food. There is a growing consensus that individuals may well assimilate nutrients quite differently. As a result, our body sensors can get confused in telling us what we need to eat because of malnutrition from inadequate or contaminated food sources (the oxymoron "junk food" is appropriate). This is another reason we need to stop long enough (and quietly enough) to listen to ourselves: We easily fall into the habit of letting our minds choose our diet because it is convenient or popular, instead of asking our body what it would like. A first step is to stop eating manufactured food, which robs food of essential nutrients, and to eat only unprocessed food.

Unprocessed food doesn't necessarily mean more work in the kitchen—canned and dried food can sometimes be healthier than that from the produce market, because food is best eaten in it's natural growing season. For example, tomatoes and melons should always be ripened on the vine; only canned tomatoes and frozen melons are likely to be vine-ripened.

Norman Shealy, M.D., a pioneer in the treatment of chronic pain, grows his own food and suggests others to do the same. (He notes that proper nutrition seems to help with relief of pain.) Neighborhood lots, vegetables in pots, gardening by the square foot all present possibilities to that. Farmer's markets, natural grocers and roadside stands offer another option. Fish frozen at sea is sometimes fresher than that which is in the market. Dried fruit keeps well, as it's grown in season and harvested at its peak because of storage costs.

I select real food from fresh, frozen, canned and dried sources preferably grown in season and harvested with love. From this wide selection of real food, I fill my cupboards and refrigerator so I may select from healthy foods at any given time.

I remember the classic study of infant nutrition by Davis where healthy babies, six to 12 months old, were given their choice of real foods and not fed a particular one until the baby reached for it; they all thrived.

Skeptics scoffed, "But you offered them a balanced diet!" Yes, Emily could have pigged out on carrots, but she didn't. She also reached for meat and cereal and maintained good nutrition and health.

I was abashed that even my cat intuitively knew what was best for herself. I have been in a power struggle with my cat. I have been feeding her dry food with an occasional tuna and "treat" of canned food, and it has done wonders for her coat. The last three months she has been refusing dry food. I have poured broth on it, "starved" her one meal, put her bowl outside—nothing worked. She stilled meowed for wet food.

Then my daughter, who knows about these things, asked how old she was.

"Eight this summer."

"You shouldn't be feeding her dry food at all. Too high in ash content. She could get serious urological problems that will mean high veterinarian bills. Feed her only canned food." So I did.

When I stopped succumbing to junk foods, I cleaned out cupboards of anything that had: 1) preservatives, 2) white processed flour, 3) white processed sugar, or 4) caffeine (except teas and chocolate). I knew if it was in the house, I would eat it. Out! Then I began to shop for real food. One guideline I followed was whether it looked like it did when God made it when it came off the vine, the tree, the bush, or the soil. (I also learned that things that looked like wholesome food might not be because of preservatives, fertilizers or insecticides.)

I learned to read labels for additives, sweeteners, or preservatives. I asked about how meat was grown and slaughtered. What was it fed? What antibiotics and hormones was it given? Did I really want to eat a piece of dead cow? How was it killed? Although kosher foods may have additives, I figure it is better to be blessed than unblessed.

I compare what I have learned to how native Americans killed and prepared their meat. On the occasions I buy meat, I give a prayer of thanksgiving for the animal which sustained my life. I have had a lot of people ask me why I do not espouse a vegetarian diet. Because of my studies in nutritional anthropology (which is based on the indigenous crops from the area where one's ancestors hailed from), I have come to believe that genetics, climate, and available food supply dictate individual needs in different ways, one consequence of which is that people will have different food intolerances. Different ethnic groups from different parts of the world have different dietary needs; for some people that includes meat.

The subject of food intolerances is a sensitive one. Allergic reactions are usually dramatic (rashes and so forth), but there are many gradations of intolerance to different foods down to the level where we just don't digest them well, and as a result are not nourished by them. The situation is also aggravated because we are exposed to so many toxic substances in water, air and our workaday world that we cannot tolerate the foods we otherwise could, if only we lived more naturally. When I am camping in the high mountains, I can comfortably eat some things that I can't bear when I am also having to resist the toxicity of city living.

I discovered in my research that some allergies/intolerances appear to be genetic and some acquired. Queen Elizabeth was said to ban tomatoes from the kingdom because of her genetically acquired intolerance to them; no Tudor could tolerate tomatoes. I have difficulty with the entire nightshade family, which also includes white potatoes and red peppers. Red potatoes, however, are fine for me.

Wheat is one of the common food allergies. When I became aware I could not tolerate the gluten in wheat, I started baking my own bread from other grains. I found that even if the label said the loaf was made from another grain (such as corn, oat or rye), that was usually only a portion. I find wheat is the primary ingredient of almost all commercially baked goods.

Rather than view bread-baking as a chore, I developed a pleasant Saturday habit of it. I now make a wide variety of breads with a simple basic method. I put all the liquids in the blender: oil, juice, water, eggs, milk, honey, maple syrup, molasses, nut butter, apple sauce, jelly cranberry sauce, ripe bananas—whatever strikes my fancy on that particular day. I put all the dry ingredients in my steel mixing bowl: rice flour, rye, corn, oat, amaranth, kamut, or spelt; baking powder, or soda, spices—ginger, cinnamon, nutmeg, salt—again, as the mood strikes me. Then I blend the wet and the dry. I add seeds, nuts or fruit and bake at 350 degrees until brown around the sides. Sample. Savor. Appreciate the results of my labor.

It was helpful to me in identifying my food intolerances to think of them in terms of family groups because eating one will often create a craving for all. For instance, one lady I know stopped smoking until she ate salsa. The hot peppers led to a craving for cigarettes and she began her smoking addiction all over again saying, "I can't stop." She could have stopped smoking if she had considered that tobacco is a member of the nightshade family.

Supplements

Ideally, we should get all nutrients we need from the food we eat. Practically speaking, that is not always the case. For instance, I have never met an obese person who was properly nourished according to amino acid assays. Often specific nutrients, water, sunlight, or love are missing. In these instances, as well as with people dealing with addictions and other states of debilitation due to illness or accident, supplements and herbs may be called for.

Just as people sometimes need the help of a physical therapist to develop an exercise program, so do they sometimes need a prescribed diet to begin a healthy food selection process. The body may be confused with its signals and cravings, especially one that is addicted, obese, toxic or ill. In my experience, it takes a knowledgeable adviser to prescribe what one needs, which includes both how much to take and how long to continue taking it. Vitamin C helps increase resistance to disease and better calcium absorption, but if it is made from corn, and one is allergic to corn, then it will not work. Amino acids can be given for depression, addictions, and obesity; trace minerals and other vitamins can be supplied for specialized disorders.

Dr. Shealy suggests we all need 800 units of Vitamin E and 3 grams of Vitamin C just to help our bodies metabolize toxins in an industrialized society. But if we are allergic to oranges, Vitamin C must come from other sources. I would suggest we consider these suggestions soberly, and make allowances for individual differences at any particular point in time. (See his book, *90 Days to Self Health.*)

Questions to ask concerning the food we ingest are:

1. Is (or was) it fresh when canned, dried or frozen?
2. Was it grown and harvested (or slaughtered) with respect for the creative process of life?
3. Is it pure, clean, free of adulteration or have poisons (preservatives) been added or nutrients unnecessarily destroyed in processing?
4. Does my body need it/want it *now?*

Occasionally it is good to step back from a normal routine. Maybe it is time to fast, eat chicken soup, drink juices, or add protein at every meal.

Water

Most of us do not drink enough water. The old rule of eight glasses a day should be modified, if need be, to include a glass of water after every healing, a glass of water every hour unless you have just eaten. More in hot climates, less in cold.

The water needs to be pure. My doctor put me on distilled water. "You have enough minerals in your system (that you would get from tap water) to last the rest of your life," he says. Well water, spring water, pure water. Water exposed to the sun is good. Drinking water helps assure sufficient hydration.

One needs to be aware of water coming out of the body to better gauge the need for water coming in. Evaporation, perspiration, and dehydration as well as urination all need to be considered. When the body has more toxicity to fight, it tends to retain water. Therefore more intake is needed for cleansing.

Use water to cleanse the body inside and out. Proper foods and hydration will cleanse the body internally. Baths and minerals will clean it externally.

I shall forever be thankful to the Romans for their engineering feats of adequate sewage and warm baths. I bathe twice daily and wash my hands before meals. I was immersed when I was baptized. I believe in water!

Harriet Coates, teacher of *Course in Miracles* and ancient wisdom, taught me years ago to wash my hands "in cold water up over the wrists after each patient. It breaks the connection." I had no idea what she meant at the time, but I knew I had more energy at the end of the day when I heeded her admonition. So I did.

Another teacher informed me that as I went through the day, I accumulated barbs and crud from my patients in my energy body and needed to bathe immediately on getting home. Again, on blind faith and as a noble experiment, I tried it, and felt more energy, slept better and continued my practice of bathing.

It has been said that immersion in mineral water breaks down the auric body and we then build a new one, fresh out of the tub, so to speak. Should immersion in water or a shower not be possible, the Essenes taught to place a damp cloth sequentially over all parts of the body.

Times for bathing are after healing work or at the end of the work day and in the morning after sleep. Sometimes, as needed or desired, I add aromatic oils, essence of flowers, salts, minerals or mud. Each has a particular function at a particular time.

For whatever reason, people have been "taking the waters" in sacred places of healing from time immemorial. In my rural childhood, we considered streams, pools and ponds as resources for bathing. Sulfur springs, radon springs, mineral springs. They each have their places in healing.

And so as we begin our physical healing, we need to assess ourselves and our lifestyle to establish our natural rhythms of healing and health.

1. Food choices, nutrition and supplements
2. Rest
3. Breathing
4. Sleep
5. Body movement
6. The earth
7. The sun

Chapter 2

Commitment

When we were beginning to realize the extent of the damage to my back after an auto accident, some authorities and well meaning friends, thinking they were being "realistic," said things like, "You'll never get over it, you'll just have to learn to live with it."

Fortunately in times like these my stubborn streak comes to the fore, I set my jaw, and think, oh yeah? That's what *you* say! All knowledge isn't discovered yet. I'll search and work and pray and we won't know how much better I can get until the day I die.

I have family stories to draw upon for that belief. My dad told the story of my grandmother who was home on the farm in Arkansas one day when one of her nephews was chopping wood: "Well, the axe slipped and he chopped two toes clean off. Someone went a running for Mary Ellen, hollering up a storm. 'Well, just quit your hollering, gather up his toes and bring me some soot off the chimney and that clean shirt hangin' there.' Whereupon she applied clean soot to toes attached and unattached. Bound them all tightly together with strips from the clean shirt, wrapped a clean petticoat around all that, gave him half a cup of whiskey, and he healed, good as new. Except he did have a black ring around both those toes the rest of his life." (This was pre-1900.)

Or the story about my cousin Slim, my Uncle Boone 's boy, who was "down" in his back something awful. Terrible pain. Couldn't do any farm work or anything. Taking to drink to ease the pain. Doctors couldn't do anything for him. Took him all the way to Oklahoma City, too. Well, seems one day when Daddy came courting Mama, he brought Slim along and they all took a joy ride in somebody's new Roadster. Roads weren't too good and before they knew it they hit a big hole in the road, bouncing them around something fierce. Hit their heads on the roof of the car and just about knocked them out. Well, all my daddy could think of was poor Slim's back!

Slim let out such a holler they were afraid he was paralyzed. They stopped the car as soon as they could and got poor Slim out of the car to lay him flat on the ground. But before they could get him lying down he suddenly stopped hollering. "Gawd almighty," he said. "My back don't hurt no more!" His back never gave him anymore trouble after that.

All the stories about healing in our family carried a moral:

"Never give up."

"Don't pay too much attention to what the experts say. Twenty years from now, they'll probably be saying something entirely different." (I liked this one.)

"Educate yourself on it."

"God moves in mysterious ways, His wonders to perform."

Some relatives went to faith healers, others to "goat doctors," so-called because they were said to drink and prescribe goat's milk. (Obviously a person allergic to dairy products from cow's milk would have remission of symptoms.) I tasted it once and decided I'd just as soon go ahead and die rather than drink goat's milk.

Coming from a background that taught me never to give up, and my own experience in overcoming physical disease, poverty, depression, and various hardships, it was natural for me to not give up on healing my back. I have a *commitment* to getting well; it's part of my family's heritage.

And, from my farming background where crops grow in a season, apple trees take years to bear fruit, and families exist in multigenerational wisdom, I am aware that healing is a process.

Sure, I'd like it to be like cousin Slim's back that was healed by a bump in the road, or Aunt Ora's "goat doctor" who got her off dairy products. But what is important is that I'm committed to the process of healing, not setting an artificial time frame.

When I fell in 1969 and dislocated my kneecap for the final time before complete surgical removal of everything to do with a knee, I was devastated. I had just moved into an old fixer-upper in Laguna Beach. I knew no one. I wanted to give the kids and me a better life after my traumatic divorce, and bam! I found myself in a cast for four weeks, mostly flat on my back. Surgery, then physical therapy for six more months. Then the prognosis: "You'll probably never have full range of motion again.

Today I do have full range of motion, though I must admit I'm a bit gimpy, especially on rainy days. But I'm still working on improving my comfort and function.

I am *committed* to my physical health and well being.

A few years back, I worked my way into a corner and got Epstein-Barr virus resulting in Chronic Fatigue Syndrome. Fought back. Educated myself. Nutrition. Allergies. Amino Acids. Conferences. Books. Recovered.

People ask me, "How do you know if what you are learning is truth?" Good question. I test by two precepts: (1) "By their fruits you shall know them", and (2) the test of time.

Here is a story of what I mean by the test of time. I wish I could eat chocolate ice cream every night before I went to bed. I actually sleep more deeply and wake up more refreshed. But after two or three days, I'll get a pimple on my nose, and after a week I'll gain three pounds. So, I've made a *commitment* to myself to eat ice cream only on Friday, in a reasonable amount.

My mother and father worked very hard all their lives, and I personally do not think I could have weathered all the hardships and privations they experienced. But they never neglected our education. Either in common sense or book learning. My mother read to us, took us to the library, fought the establishment to get me good teachers and college prep courses.

Priorities were:

1. The family and its well being.
2. God. (Surprised? My daddy always said the Bible says that the person who neglects their own family is worse than an infidel. He said that if you put your family first you are really putting God first, because God is in people.)

Commitment to family comes first for me. And through my parents' *commitment* to our family, they encouraged me to also have a *commitment* to education.

As we begin to comprehend the task of "healership", we are struck with the awesome *commitment* that is to be required of us.

Realizing that the instrument for healing is the self in its entirety, we are given pause. Is this really for me?

The first step in "healership" is a *commitment* to *Right Rhythmic Living*. Throughout the ages, healers have been prepared for their vocation through communities, monasteries, tribal customs and apprenticeships. The country doctor gave his all to his community. There was no such thing as office hours or take two aspirins and call me in the morning; doctoring was his life.

Florence Nightingale was *committed* to good hospital care. Her life was devoted to that calling.

"Healer, heal thyself."

If I don't have the *commitment* to heal myself, where can I get the wherewithal to heal others? How could I have the audacity, first of all?

Practicing Right Rhythmic Living takes us on an unknown journey. We test the outer limits of our courage to stand apart from what normative customs are; the courage to substitute our Higher Sense Perceptions for our regurgitated learning; the courage "to go where no one has gone before"—into the very core of our being into faith in following our Spirit.

This journey leads us to question our preconceived notions and cherished beliefs, and sacrifice our ego to a path of heart-centered living, loving service. It gives us the faith that there is a Higher Power to help us through. In a way, the path to "healership" is like Frank Baum's yellow brick road in the Wizard of Oz. There may be detours on the path, we may get lost, but if we keep our goals in mind—courage, a fine mind, and a loving heart—we'll not only get to the Emerald City, we'll get back Home again.

PART II

Healing Our Woundedness

Chapter 3

Emotional Clearing

"Story . . . the most precious container of the spirit."

Laurens Van der Post

A man arrived at my office, very shaken, knowing while driving home late one evening he had hit and killed a pedestrian. "I 'knew' I shouldn't have been driving after drinking that much, but nothing had ever happened before," his voice trailed off. "I understand she left two little girls . . . but they won't let me talk to anyone in the family."

Then, in a whisper, "I'm so sorry." His voice reflected his broken heart. After his story of lifelong alcoholism poured out, he quietly affirmed through his tears, "I know now I'll never drink and drive again."

And he didn't, with the help of Alcoholics Anonymous and its Twelve-Step program for living.

Alcoholism helps turn off the pain of "feeling" what we "know." The Twelve-Step program helps us get in touch with feelings and acknowledge what we knew but did not accept.

Many times, many patients, many friends, and me: We get into trouble with ourselves because we know something, but we do not "know" it.

"I knew my husband could get pretty surly when he'd drink, but he only hit me once." Her eyes carried the fear. "I guess I knew it with my head. But not here," she said, pointing to her heart.

I visited her in the hospital. She had a broken jaw, black eyes, a broken foot, and a skull fracture. She had no money and no relatives close by. In my office we'd discussed his potential for violence but she couldn't admit it to herself because she "loved him."

"Now I know," she said. "I'll never go back."

Another man 'knew' he should not lend his son money to start a business but "He needed to get on his feet somehow. I 'knew' he had no business experience." Then softly, "He went through the fifty thousand dollars in three months. He's never been able to accept authority, so I thought he could manage okay if he were his own boss." After a silent moment of reflection, "Now I *know* he can't. Please, help me, I feel so guilty for not helping him any more."

It doesn't help to try and save others from themselves when they "know" better. Some people have to go through the pain of many failures before they can acknowledge their own self-deceit. No matter how well intentioned we may be we can't save people from themselves. I helped the father see that his pattern of "rescuing" his son from the pain of immature choices was the behavior to consider. He concluded that a strong and caring father would actually withdraw his support. "I *know* now—I love him too much to contribute to his self-destructive ways."

As a psychotherapist, I have heard stories like these for 40 years. Change the sex or age of the people, alter the circumstances, and recycle the plot. Stories of human lives lost, tragedies of relationships ripped apart wrecked on the jagged rocks of fear and self-deception that lie beneath the surface of consciousness.

What happens to us? What do we do to ourselves? How to we get ourselves so messed up?

"I *know* I shouldn't do drugs. I was in parochial schools until the ninth grade. Then I went away to boarding school and started smoking marijuana. Everybody was doing it. I didn't even like it at first. Then we'd do cocaine whenever we could get it. Then I did mushrooms and nothing much happened, until the second time, last week." Her face contorted with pain, as it became real. "I haven't been able to sleep at all since then, and I feel like I'm losing my mind. I see things that I know aren't there. . . ."

Slowly she poured out the tale of her family. Seemingly perfect on the outside, filled with emotional and physical abuse behind closed doors. Unable to find acceptance in her peer group without taking drugs, she succumbed to group pressure and temporarily relieved the hidden pain.

Six months and many drugs later, she hit bottom. She checked into a hospital—first the detoxification unit, then the psychiatric ward. Finally, in a halfway house, she began to slowly rebuild her life. Filled with guilt and remorse, she now really *knew* what she already "knew."

Listening with compassion to stories like these, and helping people find the truth has been my life's work. The individuals who come to see me are crushed down by the pain of emotional suffering caused when families are broken. ("Do you come from a 'broken' home?" we ask.) They suffer the pain of broken relationships ("We broke up Saturday night"), of broken expectations ("I lost my job—the company went under"), and of poor choices ("I 'knew' I shouldn't have married her").

I've suffered from the physical pain of two spinal stress fractures and torn muscles, tendons, and ligaments. Either way, we go through the same process, of feeling our pain, sharing it, and learning new ways to cope with our suffering to facilitate our healing. Anger, frustration, and loss. Heartbreak, loneliness, and fear. Going deep within to reevaluate ourselves, our ways of thinking and doing and feeling.

Pain and suffering is not a new experience for me. I have sought psychological and spiritual help in times of family crisis and loss throughout my life. Going through the pain as I feel it in the present invariably also surfaces old hurts and wounds of previous years. Buried in the unconscious, below the surface, pain exists in a clump, like coral built up over itself through the years, forming a reef of crustations on my soul.

This morning before waking I had a dream. I was arguing

with a friend who occasionally just tunes me out. I usually figure he is just having a bad day, and back off until a later time. But in this dream I was really chewing him out. "Look!" I cried, "I'm not going to be treated this way anymore! I've had it! I don't care if I never see you again. You take, take, take, and never give back!" I slammed the door shut and was in another room with a childhood friend who had grown into an obese adult. I am uncomfortable sharing a meal with her as she eats in one sitting what I usually consume in two or three days. Waking from the dream I realized that my needy child self (the angry one) was being too demanding of my usually giving friend and was "greedy" for his attention. These feelings below the surface of consciousness would never come out in real life because I'm "such a nice person" and smart enough to know that it would also be stupid and wouldn't contribute to our relationship at all.

The dream released the emotional frustration of "neediness" in an acceptable way, and enabled me to get in touch with the "hidden hunger" that caused a "gluttony" of demands on my friend's time.

Now awake and going deep within to reevaluate the relationship, I felt less needy and more accepting of this really good friend. He had reminded me of someone I had a relationship with that didn't give me the attention I truly needed and deserved, and with whom I stayed much too long. I "knew" the old saying, "You can't make a silk purse from a sow's ear," but I didn't "wake up" and admit that this person was just a "piece of pigskin" for my expectations until years of suffering had gone by. Then I *knew* it. And I let go.

But there were still crustaceans of anger built up over years of resentment. The anger was at myself for my own neediness, my lack of judgment, and for my obstinacy in refusing to believe he was less than what I wanted him to be. The greedy, needy me was symbolized by the gluttonous childhood friend of my dream.

Realizing all this on awakening, I was greatly relieved. I relaxed at a profoundly deep level, and the back pain diminished.

The pain and frustration of not being able to lift a dinner

plate triggered an old, yet very present memory of helplessness and pain. My unconscious revealed the buried resentment in my dreams, and with awareness I could both understand and begin to forgive myself.

Today, I am better able to let go of demands on loved ones as they are balanced with appropriate expectations to have my needs for nurturing met. And I'm learning to be more discriminating in my choice of those I "love" so that my relationships can be reciprocal ones; not more "I'll give and you take" on either side.

It isn't comfortable to explore the pain of "broken" homes, "severed" relationships, "failed" marriages, or "stupid" mistakes, or to examine the haughty personal pride that has led to our shortsightedness.

That's why we need a friend on the path—a spiritual advisor, a confessor, a psychotherapist. Or a physician, a loving relative, a trusted confidant. And a relationship with our Creator, called by whatever name we hold in reverence.

As we *know* the truth of ourselves we can begin to forgive ourselves and find relief. But first we need to tell our story.

When my sister and I were children, my mother read stories to us every night before bed. My favorite fairy tales were *Snow White and Rose Red*, and later *The Princess and the Pea*. *Snow White and Rose Red* is the story of two sisters who went into the forest every day to pick berries. One day they came upon a wicked little troll who wished to do them harm. Through cunning and clever ways they managed to foil the troll.

I knew this story was true. Every word. Snow White may have been prettier, but her sister Rose Red was smarter and kept the wicked troll from hurting them. Because I identified with Rose Red and she carried a pair of scissors, I always kept my small pocketknife with me. And still do.

When I say, "You never know when you'll need to cut a troll's beard loose from a fallen log," my sister knows exactly what I mean.

The Princess and the Pea, as most everyone knows, is the story of a poor girl who comes upon a castle and asks for food and lodging for the night. The lady of the castle perceives the girl's inner goodness and puts her to bed on top of a large pile of the best mattresses. Under the bottom mattress she places a tiny pea. The next morning, when asked how she slept, the girl admits she slept poorly—there seemed to be a huge stone under her mattress. The lady embraces the girl and declares her to be the long-lost princess, for only a princess would be sensitive enough to feel the pea.

The Princess and the Pea helped me understand that I was a special person, even if others consider me "strange." This first happened in school, shortly after my family moved from Oklahoma to California. After all, I talked with a funny accent, and even basic words were different: the evening meal was "supper," and the midday meal was "dinner."

To call us in to supper, my mother would stand on the back porch and holler, "Ouuuueeee, Ouuuueeee," in descending tones—a little like the "Souuueee" sound used to call hogs on the farm. Mortified by the snickers of the other children, I asked her why she hollered so. "Sound travels farther that way, so you can hear me." Case closed.

I'd never heard of Father Junipero Serra and his famous California missions. One day at school, we were told to carve a mission from a bar of Ivory soap, but my bar kept breaking off. I was used to carving in wood and making bows and arrows. Soap was for washing! I was a failure at soap carving.

Much later, at my 30th high school reunion, I found eight other classmates who had also attended my grammar school. I was quite surprised to find that they thought I was smart and indeed, somewhat special. That knowledge helped heal the hurt of perceived rejection—from always being chosen last for sports teams, and from not having anyone regular to eat lunch with.

Clothes and fitting in with your peer group are all-important to a young girl. In grammar school I had two dresses to wear. I alternated the days I wore them, so that one week I'd wear the first dress on Monday, Wednesday and Friday and the second dress on

Tuesday and Thursday. Then I'd reverse the order the following week. I felt a little like the Little Match Girl. I thought I'd die.

In junior high skirts and sweaters were de rigueur. The "in" crowd wore cashmere sweaters and carried leather binders. I had two wool sweaters, one skirt, and several dresses. I may have been a Princess on the inside, but as yet no Lady had discovered me. Most days I despaired of ever being anything but a poverty-stricken social outcast who didn't belong anywhere outside of home.

But I did belong in my extended family. Although this family was now my mother's in Sacramento, I had deep emotional roots from my first nine years in intense involvement with my father's family in Oklahoma. We were Oklahomans, not "Okies." Every Sunday we had get-togethers. We laughed and sang and told stories. My aunts and uncles told their stories of what had happened during the week. In this group, healing hands and the significance of dreams were taken for granted.

One Sunday when we congregated at my Grandfather Jimmie's house, Aunt Iny met us at the door. "Have you heard? Papa had a dream of fish swimming upstream!" Everyone was very excited. Then began the spirited discussion of who in the family could be pregnant. The dream was absolute. Every time Papa dreamt of fish swimming upstream someone was pregnant who didn't know it yet. (It usually happened within the first three days of pregnancy.) He had never been wrong.

If someone was ill, they sent for my father. He could tell them if it was serious enough to see a doctor, as money was dear and doctor's fees were hard to come by. He'd often prescribe a folk remedy, or recommend a lifestyle change. Any sick and crying baby would immediately quiet when he held it.

One story was told repeatedly. A neighbor was "putting up" (canning in jars) some peaches and a fruit jar exploded. A sliver of glass was imbedded in her jugular vein. The back seat of the car was soaked with blood, but Marion (my father) kept his hand right on her artery until they got to the hospital. He saved her life.

Then would come a passionate discussion of my father's uncanny judgment, "most people's" stupidity, and the necessity of "doing the right thing"—not for personal reward of people, but because one was a Christian.

But my father had no truck with "faith healers."

"Bunch of quacks!" he'd say. This would start yet another heated discussion because at least two of my mother's uncles and three of her sisters were Pentecostal, and would pray over anybody at the drop of a hat, sometimes, in "tongues." These displays of religious fervor always left me a bit unnerved, and I secretly took my father's side in these religious discussions.

Stories of miraculous healing were told with great passion and utter belief. On the way home, my father would say to me quietly, "Bunch of nonsense," and my down-to-earth mother would say, "The age of miracles has passed." Nevertheless, it was a marvelous education in seeing people who loved each other very much vehemently disagree about basic beliefs.

One day I was walking home from the store with my ancient great-aunt Ella. She recounted to me matter-of-factly a story of her recent illness. She had died and gone to heaven, had passed the moon and the stars, and had seen a bright light. An angel came and told her she had to go back for a while longer. I accepted her story as gospel, and we went on to talk of ice cream.

Aunt Ella was from Missouri and would have nothing to do with the supernatural. She was just sharing her story. My child's mind accepted the story as a vehicle for truth; that is, I accepted the truth behind the words.

Monday morning all thoughts of religion, personal stories, and Oklahoma culture were put away, and I'd go back to being a poverty-stricken outcast.

Now as an adult when I "tell my story" to my therapist, spiritual director, trusted friend or beloved family member, we are both aware of a deeper meaning than the manifest content of our words. We say colloquially, "We had a meeting of the minds," or "I poured my heart out." Outward circumstances of class and culture do not circumscribe the boundaries of the soul's yearning to be understood.

The greatest tragedy to strike our family was not revealed to my conscious mind until I was almost 30 years old. After a Masters and Ph.D. in psychology, two children, and two years in therapy, I began to remember. Now grown, many of my childhood friends were also able to remember. When we were very young, a child molester had moved into the neighborhood. A picture of abuse and sexual molestation began to emerge from memories long repressed.

Not quite able to believe the images and dreams that were emerging, I sought out a former neighbor for whom I used to baby sit. She never went to church, always wore slacks, and drank beer from a can. But she was a straight shooter; I could depend on her to tell the truth.

"Whatever happened to the Smiths?" I asked her. "They moved so suddenly."

She was surprised I didn't know. Seems "he got" one of the neighborhood children. The child managed to break free and ran home to tell her father and show him what happened. Her father was from the Old Country and was going to kill the man, but my neighbor talked him out of it. She convinced him that going to the electric chair wouldn't solve the problem. Instead she herself confronted the Smiths and gave them three days to move or the father would take matters into his own hands. The Smiths were gone 36 hours later.

I later learned that they had moved to a new house across from a grammar school. Those were the days before rape hot lines, before self-help groups for adults molested as children or child protective services. Shame and guilt kept such secrets hidden, although brave adults sometimes delivered vigilante justice.

But for the loving support of a large network of family and friends, I, too, could have been one of the "lost ones." As the long-buried fear began to surface through dreams and therapy, I was able to heal many of the frightful wounds.

My subconscious *knew* what my conscious mind didn't. I endured years of fear, anxiety, and depression that became attached to other people and objects. For instance, I was afraid of spiders. When my son was born, I washed his diapers and hung them in the sun to dry. Bringing them indoors to fold them one day, I saw a spider. I ran from the room in sheer terror, unable to go back until my young and fearless husband came home from work, found it, killed it, and took it back outside.

I didn't realize until my therapy that, at a symbolic level, the spider reminded me of a long-forgotten fear.

After a person has "told their story" on a conscious level, I say, "Tell me your dream." If they answer, "I don't dream," I point out that dream lab studies show that we all dream; it's just that some of us don't remember the dreams. "As your therapy proceeds, you will begin to remember your dreams—probably when you first wake up. It helps to write down even the slightest remembrance."

Eventually one memory will trigger another as we explore the dream and its symbolic meaning. Other dreams will begin to surface, often dreams from childhood. "I had this dream, and I suddenly remembered that I used to have one like it when I was a child."

Understanding dreams is akin to understanding *The Princess and the Pea.* It is a coded message. Only as we get in touch with the emotions involved does it begin to make sense.

Adults who do not remember childhood abuse and assault often begin to remember first in nightmares. They may awaken "scared stiff." Only the courageous continue therapy. Others descend into drugs, alcohol, or promiscuity. Or they turn off their feelings altogether. What they don't know is that they are attempting to stop the pain of their own inner, hurt, bewildered child buried within, but it doesn't work this way.

First we must stop the destructive, running-away behavior with the support of God and trusted friends. Within this context we draw courage to exorcise the demons of our childhood fears. Dreams are often the first step toward remembrance. Remember how everything is connected to everything else?

An attorney came to me for help in recovering from a "failed" marriage. As therapy progressed, we also discovered he was an alcoholic, a workaholic, and further abused his body through insufficient sleep, lack of exercise, and poor nutrition. Not surprisingly, his once thriving law practice was in a shambles—he was morally bankrupt.

He suffered from hypertension, headaches, and estrangement from children now nearly grown. On the fast track to "success," he was a failure at living. As he began to face his dilemma, to live in a more healthy way, and to take an honest, courageous look at himself, he described this dream:

There is a dangerous, psychotic person in a hospital being seen by student residents in psychiatry. They don't really know how dangerous the patient is. A supervising psychiatrist is brought into the case who does realize the seriousness of the situation, and tells the students to "get their act together."

"What is the dream telling you?" I ask.

"Well, I guess I've been pretty dangerous to myself, and all the self-help things I tried to do to help myself really didn't cut it. I can't do it by myself. I need your help to cut the crap and realize the serious mess I've gotten myself into."

As we further explored how he might be "dangerous" to himself, he confessed episodes of heart pain he had been ignoring. A physical checkup did indeed show hypertension and cardiovascular distress. "I was crazy to ignore those symptoms," he said.

As he continued medical treatment we began to explore the stressors in his life, especially those at work and those he brought into his dreams. In one, he is frightened and feels very alone:

"I bring a small handgun to help the good guys get away from the bad guys. But the bad guys come in with a machine gun. They don't know that I am the one who can "crack the case." I act innocent about the handgun. They destroy it and ask if there is anything explosive in my briefcase. I shrug my shoulders as if I don't know. They shoot it with the machine gun and leave.

"The police come and search everything. They find bank notes that look like big stamps at the bottom of my briefcase. They really aren't mine, but I say they are receipts from clients that I haven't deposited in the bank yet, and they buy that story.

I really haven't done anything wrong, but it's too complicated to explain, and I'm afraid they would think I was receiving "stolen goods."

I'm sitting there stunned, and a secretary appears from no where. I have to get rid of the bank notes, and she suggests we go to the bank and set up a trust account, as we can't trust the police. I thank her for appearing just in time to help me."

As we pondered the significance of the dream, he broke down and cried. In his financial crisis, he has "borrowed" money from one of the trust accounts. It was very hard for him to trust me enough to reveal this indiscretion.

We discussed his own feeling of inadequacy (represented by the handgun) when confronted with the power of the "mob." He felt overwhelmed ("shot down") at work (the briefcase) by the un-reasonable demands he placed on himself and by the demands that he felt others place on him as well. The demands are so great he couldn't trust himself to "police" himself, and he succumbed to the temptation to borrow from the "trust account."

In the dream, I am represented by a secretary who suggests he deposit the funds in a safe place. The secretary could also be his own nourishing self-beginning to kick in and help him out of his dilemma.

After some discussion of his moral dilemma, he suggested he could execute a legally binding promissory note (with interest) for the funds he "borrowed." He did this. Freed from the pressures of wrong living, pressures that he himself caused, and living in a healthier way, his blood pressure began to normalize.

As he began to trust himself, more of his depression was lifted. One day he came into my office smiling and reported that he'd had a dream. "And I think I know what it means!" he exclaimed.

I'm in a monastery-type setting. I know many of the Brothers, but the house is like my house, even though it doesn't look like it. The Broth-ers are helping me. One changes a light bulb, another refers a client to me. They all try to help. Things are a little confusing and awkward and don't always work, but they mean well, and we are going forward in spite of my mix-ups and awkwardness.

We discussed how he is getting "his own house" in order as he sought enlightenment (the light bulb) from his Higher Power, or spiritual self. He was more in tune with his own positive attributes, and though he was clumsy in applying his new attitudes and habits, he did feel a sense of progress, of going forward.

Dora came to my office impeccably groomed, gracious, and beautifully dressed in the latest style. Her marriage of twenty-odd years was failing, her children had left home for college, her husband was a workaholic and her life was empty. She was clinically depressed. (She was not the wife of the attorney that I just described, but she could have been.)

Dora was the ideal corporate wife; her home was decorated with great skill and taste, and she belonged to the "right" clubs and volunteer organizations. After we had time to get acquainted and trust had been built between us, she told me about a frightening nightmare.

There was a fire in her house, and all her valuables went up in smoke. By the time the firemen got there, the fire was blazing throughout the house. Dora barely got out alive.

"But how did the fire spread so fast?" she asked. The firemen pointed out that plastic is made of petroleum and burns hot and quickly.

"What does the dream mean to you?" I asked gently.

"Plastic isn't real. It isn't alive like wood and ceramic. I need to take the plastic out of my house, take the 'unreal' out of my psychological house. It's time to move out of the plasticity of my life and be totally honest with myself."

She smiled ruefully. "I guess I'm like that old song, 'Laughing on the outside, crying on the inside. . . .'"

As we explored her life honestly she was able to see that fears from her past had landed her in a bad marriage. And fears of the present ("How could I support myself?") kept her there.

The plastic represented Dora's feelings of inner "death." But plastic burns hot and fast. The fire inside her "house" symbolized her repressed rage over what had become an intolerable living situation. She had to drain off her anger, remove the "plastic" from her "house" (from herself), before she could trust herself to make wise decisions about her life.

In Dora's case, staying in an abusive home as a teenager with no place to go established a pattern of subservience for survival. She projected her anger onto her husband and did not feel real as she played the role of wife and mother. These feelings were related to the years of stored up anger at her abusive father. Subservience had gotten mixed up with survival.

Massage, meaningful work, and service groups augmented her therapy to help her become real. One day, about a year later, she came in smiling.

"Remember that dream I had? About the burning plastic in my house? And I said I had to become real instead of plastic? Well, I just came across this children's story about the Velveteen Rabbit. . . ."

Redemption through suffering. I tell my clients that therapy hurts, but not going through therapy hurts more.

The woman whose husband beat her up couldn't say enough about the kind policewoman who took her report, or the policeman who visited her in the hospital. The man who killed an innocent pedestrian found the courage to go into therapy with the encouragement of family and friends.

The young woman who needed help getting off drugs had heard me speak with compassion at her high school and felt I was someone she could trust. You have to hurt more in everyday life than you do in therapy to have the courage to heal.

Expressing Our Hurts

Emotional cleansing is a painful process. But the peace inside that is gained is well worth the price. As my physical therapist friends tell me, "No pain, no gain."

Just as I needed a physical therapist to teach me new habits and new ways of using my body, I also needed to evaluate my emotions and my self-destructive ways of thinking. Some were things I did, and some were things I didn't do. Some things I "knew" but did not *know*.

As Shakespeare expressed in Hamlet's soliloquy, we humans are subject to "the slings and arrows of outrageous fortune." When we experience physical or emotional hurts, and we are members of a loving community, we normally reach out to share them and receive help in healing them.

When hurts are not given the loving attention they need as they occur, they are stored up, and require healing another day. Stored up too long, closed off, bottled up, they begin to fester, and we close up like the water-tight compartments of a torpedoed submarine. We save our ship, but we've damaged our ability to feel with a full range of emotion. We are unable to intellectually process certain events, and we've impaired our capacity to consistently function with good judgment. The healthy way to heal our hurts is to express our emotions as soon as we are hurt.

An example: Right after I had an accident, I phoned two friends. One came to see me right away and the other took me to the doctor. I was able to reach out and ask for immediate help because when I was ill for several years as a child, my family had responded to my feelings and physical ailments. Even when they couldn't help, I knew they cared.

Children who receive compassionate, caring responses to their hurts are able to learn to deal with the "slings and arrows of outrageous fortune" and "all the ills the flesh is heir to."

One year while working on my doctorate, I supervised the three-year-old group of the University's Child Development Laboratory. On occasion a child would fall down and get a nasty bump, cry a little, and then resume playing. But when Mommy or Daddy arrived at the end of the day, the child would display the hurt and burst into tears. A wise parent would examine the injury, *no matter how minor*, express concern appropriate to the hurt, and offer sympathy and reassurance *as if the accident had just occurred*. The hurt and fear would be healed immediately, and that parent would take home a happy child.

The hurt and fear that the child had bottled up for two or three hours had been released in the *now*. When hurt is released in an atmosphere of care and concern, healing occurs on many levels. Studies have shown that even the immune system responds favorably to such care. As the parent showed concern, the child released the hurt and fear that continued to exist in the eternal *now* and healing could begin.

Sometimes when parents were fatigued or burdened with their own hurts, they would say, "Oh come on, don't cry. That happened hours ago. Don't be a baby."

Later, a parent may not even know that something painful has occurred, because the child seldom talks anymore about his or her hurts.

When the release of emotion is denied at or near the time it is felt or experienced, that feeling is locked up in an increasingly watertight compartment, like coral. As we add more coral to protect the self, our ability to cope and to feel is diminished.

Sometimes it simply isn't safe to express our hurts, and we have to find ways to get along until it is safe. During some of my times of great pain and loneliness, I have withdrawn into myself for long periods of reflection and contemplate my life much as Longfellow expressed in his poem, "My Lost Youth":

> There are things of which I may not speak;
> There are dreams that cannot die;
> There are thoughts that make the strong heart weak,
> And bring a pallor into the cheek

And a mist before the eye,
And the words of that fatal song
Come over me like a chill:
"A boy's will is the wind's will,
And the thoughts of youth are long, long thoughts."
". . . My heart turns back to wander there. . . ."

With pain comes a turning within until it is safe to reach out. Reaching deeper within and sharing my pain with a like-minded soul whose life has also been etched with pain helps me to reflect on the "long, long thoughts." The reflection leads to a **knowing** and once again I am in touch with my heart. As tears cleanse my pain, they also begin to dissolve the coral on my soul and psyche.

Spending time alone with nature and getting in touch with its rhythms helped me get back in step with myself. I've always loved the mountains and the sea. For almost 30 years I lived a short walk from the Pacific Ocean. When caught in the depths of despair and thinking long, long thoughts, I'll walk to the beach and experience the rhythm of the tide. The pounding surf drowns out my cares and somehow I feel cleansed, renewed, "though I know not how."

Song and verse best express the agony and healing of my heart. Again I turn to Longfellow for solace:

The sea awoke at midnight from its sleep,
And round the pebbly beaches far and wide
I heard the first wave of the rising tide
Rush onward with uninterrupted sweep;
A voice out of the silence of the deep,
A sound mysteriously multiplied
As a cataract from the mountain's side,
Or roar of winds upon a wooded steep.
So comes to us at times, from the unknown
And inaccessible solitudes of being,
The rushing of the sea-tides of the soul;

And inspirations, that we deem our own,
Are some divine foreshadowing and foreseeing
Of things beyond our reason or control.
". . . So when storms of wild emotion
Strike the ocean
Of the poet's soul, erelong
From each cave and rocky fastness,
In its vastness,
Floats some fragment of a song. . . ."

And so we begin to get in touch with our "wild emotions" and the "vastness of the rocky fastness" of the hurts partitioned away in our unconscious mind, hidden in clumps of muscle tension and expressing themselves in discomfort and disease.

When an emotion is not released, it often gets bound up in the body and physical illness can occur.

I once had a patient who suffered from extremely painful dermatitis. It wasn't responding to standard medication. Through hypnosis she was able to find the unconscious reason for the rashes. "It's the hurts I have inside. They have to be expressed somehow, so they break out on my skin so I can see and feel them." As she learned to externalize her internal psychic pain, to get her hurts to the outside, the rashes subsided.

Sometimes we equate the ocean with the unconscious. Certainly at the symbolic level there are mysteries, dangers, and beauties that lurk below the surface of consciousness.

But there is no shortcut to emotional clearing. There is only the courage to plunge beneath the surface of consciousness. We do this with the help of compassionate guides and teachers, knowing, trusting, then *knowing* that we can chart the waters of buried hurts and come up with our own buried treasures.

With the faith that *healing will occur* as we feel, share, and go through the pain, we can then know the mystery of its sacred promise.

"So comes to us at times, from the unknown
And inaccessible solitudes of being,
The rushing of the sea tides of the Soul
And inspirations, that we deem our own,
Are some divine foreshadowing and foreseeing
Of things beyond our reason or control."

—Henry Wadsworth Longfellow

Not only does the unconscious mind hide rocky shoals of coral encrustation, it also carries within it the inspiration for healing our own wounds. Like the salamander, we carry inside a capacity of self-rejuvenation that is beyond our reason or control.

How do you select a therapist, a teacher, or a spiritual guide to help you?

Carl Rogers was a great American psychologist whose work in the '50s brought the *person* back into theories of therapy. He taught that a therapist needs to provide a safe haven and must carry an attitude of "unconditional positive regard" if emotional healing is to occur.

Here, then, are the four critical attributes of healers and teachers:

1. An attitude of unconditional positive regard
2. An understanding heart
3. The ability to establish a safe place for the feeling of old hurts
4. Intelligent compassion

In this environment, the inner abilities of the person to heal can be nourished into fruition.

Next comes background and training. Some people, like my father, are natural healers. A friend recently said to me, "As I get better I am aware of the limitations of my therapist intern, but he has such a good heart and really cares that I've been able to go into my pain." But most of us need our own therapy from well trained as well as compassionate doctors, therapists and spiritual guides.

As you begin your emotional clearing with a person you trust, with a prayer of your faith, or in a self-help group, there are several things to look for and techniques that may help. First, do you feel safe with the person or group you're with? Do they come from the heart? Do they genuinely care about your welfare? Or do they have a hidden agenda, or something they want from you? Are they into power games or looking good? Do they have a stock answer for everything?

Are they open to improvement? Do they cry, laugh, get appropriately angry? Do they allow the humanness to show? Do they admit mistakes and compensate for wrongs? Are they forgiving of themselves and other? Do they carry a grudge? Do they have a sense of humor?

Can they speak for themselves or are they always quoting others? Can they say, "My understanding is . . . ?" Or do they "know" all the truth there is to know? Do they say all the right things, but you get a weird feeling when you are with them? Do they smile all the time? How do you *really* feel when you are with them? And after you leave?

We need a safe place, an understanding heart, and someone who has charted the waters of their own unconscious if we are to heal by telling them our stories. We need to release the emotion, not perpetuate it.

In the context of a healing, supportive environment, many worthwhile techniques are helpful. Physical exercise, walking on the earth, spending time with nature and getting in touch with those rhythms are of great benefit. So are water therapy, physical therapy, massage, and meditation.

A guided meditation that I've developed and found to be almost universally helpful is the "Lake Meditation," inspired by universal healing archetypes. It uses relaxation, focusing of the mind, and imagery. It begins with breathing and a preliminary exercise called the "Light Meditation."

For those who have never meditated before, breathing begins as an exercise. Deep breathing is practiced five minutes before getting up in the morning, and five minutes after getting into bed at night. Then deep breathing is practiced for one to three minutes every hour. I've found that this will lead to breathing deeply every time I'm upset or in any kind of physical or emotional pain.

Here is one way to do the Light Meditation.

"While relaxed and breathing deeply, imagine a white light above your head, shining down upon you, enlightening your mind, and enveloping your entire body in a cocoon of white, glowing light. Begin to breathe that light slowly, deeply, and completely. Breathe it into your lungs and your belly. Breathe in the light and let go of the tension.

Breathe the light into any part of the body that holds tension or pain. It is most helpful if this breathing is practiced in the presence of a therapist or trusted friend. Specific memories often come forth, and the therapist can help. Talking about the pain of the past with someone of compassionate heart will help the emotional clearing. The purpose of the meditation is not to zone out, tune out, or anesthetize ourselves. It is to help us feel our pain so we may let it go.

Before, during and after sharing our pain, we relax our physical bodies more easily and permanently. Just as a wise hiker carries water and basic nutrients for the journey, it is good to have a cleansing, healing meditation that can nourish the mind, draining off old hurts, angers, and fears that do not necessarily need to be brought onto the conscious level. Old hurts can be dissolved by the concentration of the mind coupled with deep relaxation of the body.

How? Begin with surrounding your body with light, affirming the power of light, and then mentally directing the light to each part of your body.

Continue by sending light and relaxation to each part of your body as it is named. Stay awake so that you may consciously relax each part of your body. Relaxation means complete absence of activity or movement in that part of the body, since movement means that muscles are contracting. It is also the opposite of holding any part rigid. By doing this, you can discover the interlinking of the body and the mind, how they are connected and how one affects the other. By means of mental processes, you can learn to control many things in the body we never realized were possible.

Staying awake, take your mind over to your right foot. Send relaxation and light to each part as I name it. Relax the toes, instep, heel, calf, knee, thigh, and the hip. Make sure your right leg is completely relaxed. Relax as completely as you can. Hold your attention to the sensation and the feeling of relaxation in the entirety of your right leg. Feel the relaxation become deeper and deeper as you say to yourself, "My entire right leg is heavy and warm, absorbing the light."

Now become aware of your left foot. Relax and send light to your toes, instep, heel, calf, knee, thigh, and the hip. Make sure that your left leg is relaxed as deeply as you can. Hold your attention to the sensation and the feeling of relaxation in your left leg. Feel the relaxation become deeper and deeper as you say to yourself, "My left leg is heavy and warm, absorbing the light."

Now take your mind over to your right hand, concentrate on it. Send a command of relaxation and light to the fingers, thumb, palm, wrist, forearm, elbow, upper arm, and shoulder. Make sure your right arm is completely relaxed. Relax it as deeply as you can. Hold your attention to the sensation and feeling of relaxation in your right arm. Feel every muscle, nerve, joint, and tissue in your right arm relaxing. Feel the relaxation become deeper and deeper as you say to yourself, "My right arm is heavy and warm, absorbing the light."

Now take your mind over to your left hand and send a command of relaxation to it. Send light to your fingers, thumb, palm, wrist, forearm, elbow, upper arm, and shoulder. Make sure that your left arm is completely relaxed. Relax it as deeply as you can. Hold your attention to the sensation and feeling of relaxation in your left arm. Feel every muscle, nerve, joint, and tissue in your left arm relaxing. Feel the relaxation become deeper and deeper as you say to yourself, "My left arm is heavy and warm, absorbing the light."

Now both your arms and your legs are completely relaxed. Make sure to keep them relaxed as you bring your concentration to the base of your spine. Work your way up the spine, vertebrae by vertebrae, relaxing the muscles into the surface. Feel your back melt in the surface; your lower back, your middle back, your upper back. Release all tension from it. Imagine your spine is like a hollow tube, with light from the tip to the top, and the nerves that extend out from your spine carry this light to every organ of your body—your reproductive organs, your organs of elimination and digestion, intestines and stomach, bladder, kidneys, liver, gall bladder, adrenals, lungs, and especially your heart, your loving heart. Breathe deeply.

As you continue to breathe the light, relax your neck. Let all the muscles in your neck relax completely. First the back of your neck, then the front of your neck. Let your head rest gently and feel all the muscles in the back of your neck relaxing. Just let them go and carry on letting them go as you say to yourself, "My neck and shoulders are heavy and warm, absorbing the light." Breathe deeply.

Now become aware of your face. Relax your chin, your jaw. Let your jaw drop so that your teeth are apart. Relax your tongue, cheeks, and eyes. There is no tension in your eyes or the muscles around your eyes. Just let all tension release from the muscles in your forehead. Feel all the muscles in your face relaxing. There is no tension in your facial muscles at all as you relax your scalp. Feel that relaxation in the muscles around your head. Breathe deeply.

Now relax your chest and every time you breathe out, relax a little more. Breathe the light. Let your body sink into the floor a little more each time until the muscles, nerves, and organs in your chest and abdomen relax completely. Relax the muscles in your stomach and abdomen. Breathe deeply.

Now your body is completely and totally relaxed. There are no tensions anywhere in your body. Make sure not to move your body at all unless necessary for comfort. Stay in the state of relaxation."

In this state, emotions that are blocks to love can be released.

Release them. Anxiety, fear, insecurity, anger, hate, envy, repressed greed, possessiveness, and attachment.

Out pours the pain. In pours relief. We don't avoid old hurts; we go into the pain in order to release it.

With some people, the Light Meditation begins to heal hurts in the unconscious mind without first surfacing to the conscious mind, especially when there's been trauma or severe wounding. That's perfectly all right.

It is common for dreams to begin at this point. Sometimes there are nightmares, buried hurts surfacing in symbolic language. It is helpful to keep a dream journal when such dreams begin, and it is sometimes advisable to share them with a well-grounded person who understands dream symbols.

A dream study group made up of like-minded souls can be of great benefit. It's important to remember, though, that a group tends to sink to its lowest common denominator. It is critical that we feel safe with a group of well grounded people who aspire to right rhythmic living, for this is the group with whom we'll share material that may be too scary for the conscious mind to handle.

Sometimes it's enough to dream, journal, and share. It's sometimes wise to choose a therapist to help, one with a good heart, an open mind, and great compassion.

Sensate Focus Meditation

After you are comfortable with the breathing meditation and have selected a teacher/therapist/spiritual guide, you may be ready to clear emotions bound up in the physical body with a technique called Sensate Focus. This is the sequel to the Lake Meditation and will clear the surface tensions of daily frustrations. It is another way of listening to your body, of accessing hurts stored in your unconscious mind and is to be explored only by the brave. It should not be attempted alone any more than climbing Mt. Everest without a trusty Sherpa guide should be attempted alone. Good therapists are adept at helping you get in touch with and let go of painful memories in an appropriate time frame. They are especially helpful if material comes up that is too frightening or puzzling to handle alone.

During this meditation we learn to release the physical tension bound up in clumps of muscle tissue. In Lewis Thomas' book, *Lives of the Cell*, we learn that every cell has memory. It's probably more accurate to say that the subtle emotional energy body that penetrates the physical tissue carries the memory, if we agree with energy-based theories.

In any case, we know from Barbara Brown's seminal research on biofeedback, *New Mind, New Body*, that the feedback loop goes both ways. As the emotions are released with a person who cares, the physical body relaxes. And, as the body relaxes through massage, exercise, and breathing meditations, emotions may be released.

Here's how to do the Sensate Focus Meditation.

Get in a comfortable position in a quiet room with your arms and legs uncrossed, your eyes closed, and begin the breathing meditation. Breathe the light.

Breathe deeply. Then become aware of the sensations of your body. After noticing all the sensations, select one that is most persistent or that you feel safe exploring.

Concentrate on the sensation—pain, tension, heat, chill, itching, burning, whatever it may be. Breathe rapidly. Soon associations come to mind. Perhaps images, memories, or words. Stay with the sensation. Let the images and words pass by. Keep your attention on the feeling. Then let the images develop. Let your mind free associate.

When you have gone far enough, write it down. If you don't have words, express your feeling in some other art form—fingerpainting, crayons, pastels, oils, acrylics, pencil, watercolors—whatever medium feels appropriate to the occasion. You may choose sculpting, playing music, singing, or dance. When you are finished, work out any excess tension in physical activity. It's best if this activity is constructive, such as pulling weeds or mopping floors, so you'll feel a sense of accomplishment when you're done.

Share your memories with one of an understanding heart during the process. Write in your journal later. No matter how difficult or painful the associations, are, remember: You lived through it once, you'll live through it again. Let the emotions resurface. Let the tears flow. Speak the angry words out loud. No one can hurt you now. It is safe to feel. Stay with the emotion as it gradually releases and subsides. Finish your meditation by filling your body with light where the pain was or continues to be.

If you are alone, allow yourself 30 to 90 minutes of quiet time. Take a nap, if you can. Then let go the contacts for a while—a day or a week. Take time to heal and integrate your healed self with the rest of you. Share sparingly and judiciously. Journal your dreams. Let laughter return as you find joy in living through the pain. You will find, as I did, that there is light at the end of the tunnel, and it is not an oncoming train.

Chapter 4

Mental Clearing

> "It is good to tame the mind, which is often
> difficult to hold in and flighty, rushing wherever
> it listeth; a disciplined mind brings happiness."
>   Buddhist Scriptures

Recently, a former patient came back to me who wished more therapy to assist in changing his cognitive processes. We had worked on clearing his physical and emotional selves to a significant degree, and he had a commitment to both his healing and his optimal functioning.

He remarked how much more clearly he was able to think and how much more effective he was in functioning as CEO for a major company since his therapy. He had learned to use meditation and self hypnosis to relax and solve problems rather well, but still found himself being anxious and thinking fearful thoughts during a recent economic downturn. A major purchaser had defaulted on a bill and there was insufficient cash flow to pay current bills. Bankruptcy was a possibility.

"Help me transcend my anxiety so I may think more clearly and solve problems on an ongoing basis, one day at a time," he requested.

He knew what he wanted to do but he lacked the skills in how to achieve his goal. As the New England native told the lost tourist, "You can't get there from here."

It is normal to experience a degree of anxiety when there is a problem that does not readily lend itself to an easy solution. Studies of the effect of anxiety on test taking show that with a little anxiety most people tended to perform at a higher level, but with too much anxiety, performance diminished to levels below even that of no anxiety.

Prolonged high levels of anxiety usually lead to not only diminished performance, but poor interpersonal relationships, a decrease in self-esteem, and are a precursor to health problems: We get sick.

In the chapter on emotional clearing we found that old emotional hurts placed on current happenings lead to irrational conclusions. Examples of irrational thinking that come to mind are:

1. "If I get married, I won't love her anymore." (Love deepens with marriage; only infatuation fades.)
2. "If I have to sell my house after the divorce, I'll just shrivel up and die." (I knew a couple who had outgrown each other, both had formed other relationships of long standing but neither wished to give up the house and neither one could afford it. You would have thought it was Tara from *Gone With the Wind*.)
3. "If I just keep quiet, everything will be all right." (When actually sometimes speaking out is all that can save us.)

Emotional Clearing on an Ongoing Basis

In looking at irrational thoughts, the first consideration is to ask if more emotional clearing is in order.

In working with a therapist, one can use the same technique as with sensate focus to uncover the emotional roots of such irrational beliefs. Only instead of concentrating on the physical sensation, we focus on the irrational thought.

For example, hold the thought, get in touch with whatever emotion or physical sensation comes with it, and allow the internal stimulus to carry you to a previous traumatic experience—to be felt, spoken, shared, journalized, dreamt, and perhaps expressed in an art form of your own choosing.

With further emotional clearing we can now look more realistically at the current situation and, with hope, live it more realistically. After discharging the emotion and coming to grips with the false belief, one then speaks out loud a *true* statement, i.e.:

"I can marry her *and* our love can grow."
"I can sell my home *and* live better than I'm living now."
"I have a better chance for survival if I speak up appropriately."

When we are plunged into a state of high anxiety, we generally have a basic instinctive repertoire of responses to choose from: 1) freeze; 2) flight; 3) fight.

To freeze is appropriate when being mauled by a bear. Thinking you are dead, he'll probably give up and move on before he damages any vital organs. But rarely is our situation that serious in modern society.

Flight is appropriate when a speeding car is coming toward you. Sometimes we need to get out of the way. But running away rarely solves problems.

To fight is reasonable if you have a better chance of surviving if you take an aggressive or, when possible, assertive stand. Even a mouse will fight if cornered. In our civilized society, this generally means speaking up. Someone once said that all that is necessary for civilization to fall is for good people to say nothing in the face of injustice. We need to be aware of our normal physiological reactions to stress and to consider to what extent our flight, fight and freeze reactions are usually appropriate.

Sometimes we do the same old thing out of habit. Then we need to take a good hard look at the reality of the *current* situation and begin to change our behavioral responses to more adequately fit the situation at hand. We begin by asking the question, "How bad is it?"

There is a difference in dealing with the resultant fear that comes from an *immediate* threat and that of an ongoing perceived threat to survival, which can be physical, economic, or the loss of love—almost a spiritual survival. These days, we have the luxury of time, to clear our minds and think with the great poets and thinkers. How do I deal with this suffering, this loss?

There were some days during the worst of my pain that I must confess I returned to the book of Job in the Old Testament and commiserated with old Job. Not only was he covered with boils, but he lost his wife and children and lands and goods, and his three best friends turned against him and told him to "curse God and die."

Somehow, reading about Job gave me courage to persevere in the face of adversity. Old Job is just telling it like it is. And in times of trouble, so do we need to do likewise. He didn't sit and speak benign platitudes: "It's all for a reason . . ." "Go with the flow . . ." "Oh boy, bad karma!"

Believe me, when anyone uttered these platitudes in my presence in those early dark and painful days, I wanted to throw up.

I didn't know why I was suffering. I still don't understand all the reasons for pain and suffering in this world. And I don't like it one bit, but I was honest about my suffering.

I think there are times in life when we need to admit we don't understand the mysteries of the universe, especially of pain, suffering, and redemption. There are just some things we don't understand. Job challenges the "human wisdom" of his friends with God's mysteries.

> "Has thou commanded the morning since thy day and caused the dayspring to know his place? Has thou entered into the springs of the sea, or has thou walked in the search of the depth? Have the gates of death been opened to you?"
>
> Job 38:12

Well, no.

Accepting the mystery, we can know that the Phoenix has risen from the ashes. We know the end of the story, the resolution of the mystery.

And Job prayed for his friends—his stupid, arrogant, false friends—and the Lord restored him to health and gave him twice as much as he had before. So Job died, "being old and full of days."

Only as we are honest with ourselves and others about both the situation *and* the magnitude of our suffering or despair are we prepared to move on.

Only as we admit our suffering *and* that we don't understand why, that the answer is beyond human understanding can we also, *at the same time*, have hope.

Hope as a Response to Anxiety

In my darkest days I would remember the story of Job, admit it was beyond my understanding and remember also the admonition, "Hope thou in God." And I would remember the sacred scripture from the Hebrew prophet Habbakuk (3:17)

> Although the fig tree shall not blossom,
> Neither shall fruit be in the river
> The labor of the olive shall fail
> And the fields shall yield no wheat
> The flock shall be cut off from the fold
> And there shall be no herd in the stall
> Yet I will rejoice in the Lord
> I will rejoice in the God of my salvation.

Now, for a farmer, a man dependent on the land and the harvest for his survival, that's a true statement of hope.

After we have taken a look at our anxiety and our misery and evaluated it in light of the past and the present magnitude of the situation; after we have come to grips with the truth of our feelings and expressed them to an understanding person who loves us, we can then begin to think more clearly in order to solve the problem. Such an attitude opens the door of the mind to rational thinking so that realistic problem solving can begin.

Sometimes the *big* problem is too overwhelming for our finite minds to deal with. Then we may need to adopt the problem-solving techniques known as "partialize the problems." That is, take it one step at a time.

A friend was in the hospital. She had just given birth to her second child. Her disabled mother who lived at home with her was reported missing (she had Alzheimer's disease). When her husband came to visit he told her he wanted a divorce.

Overwhelming.

Good social worker that she was by profession, and aware of her feelings of being overwhelmed, she *thought* to herself immediately:

"PARTIALIZE the PROBLEM."

How?

1. She picked up the phone and called the police to report her mother as missing. Then she called a social worker to make an appropriate placement when she was found, fortunately less than 30 minutes later. She simply couldn't care for her at home anymore. (Problem solving.)

2. She told her husband he could leave, but if he didn't pay all the house bills and the babysitter for the oldest child he would have such a lawsuit on his hands he would think those bills were peanuts. And to have all his things moved out before she got home, or he'd never see them again. (Assertive.)

3. She phoned the bank and asked them to freeze the bank account. (Problem solving.)

4. She phoned her boss and asked her to recommend a divorce lawyer. (Problem solving.)

5. She called the lawyer and told him what she had done and asked him to draw up the necessary papers. (Problem solving)

6. She called her priest and asked him to come to the hospital and pray for her and to set a date to baptize the baby. (Assertive.)

7. *Then* she cried and called a friend to share her feelings. (Catharsis.)

Sometimes we need to handle a problem before we allow its emotional expression to take place.

In my case, when my husband asked for divorce I went to my therapist, shared my feelings, and *he* sent me to *his* attorney.

Maybe that's the difference in approaches between a social worker and a psychologist. We each have our own coping styles and need to approach problem solving in our own individual ways. (Note that we both sought expert help.)

Another time when I was in a crisis I went to see my spiritual advisor. His first question was "Do you have a good lawyer?" Assured that I did, he heard my fears, and *then* we prayed. We prayed for wisdom, for strength to persevere, and for openness to guidance, knowing that God is with us.

Then he laughed (and I was able to laugh with him), at our human fears and frailties, *while at the same time* considering my dire straits, and his from the past.

Maintaining a Field of Mental Calm

Just as a car runs better if there is preventative maintenance, so do we think better if we maintain healthy habits of thinking. In the Lake Meditation we imagined filling our bodies with light after releasing the tension stored there. When we find a meditation we need to fill our minds with "hopeful thoughts" rather than "fear thoughts."

How do we break the habit of "fear thoughts", of projecting into the future? For instance:

- What will happen if I don't find a job before my unemployment runs out?
- What will happen if she dies?
- What will happen if _____?

When a fear thought occurs that is beyond the problem solving technique approach and we are just scaring ourselves with a worst-case scenario, we need to change our thinking habits. It is essential to discipline one's thoughts to correct one's thinking. Self-discipline is the key for current *constant* worry thoughts. We can learn to use what is called "thought stoppage."

A friend taught me this technique when I was experiencing Epstein-Barr, a virus that causes Chronic Fatigue Syndrome, which leads to debilitating fatigue. I was thinking, "What if I never get well?"

"When a fear thought occurs, immediately imagine yourself pulling a weed from your garden and substitute a flower thought. You may wish to begin by weeding your garden every morning for five minutes as a part of your morning meditation."

After a week of practice, I was able to successfully weed my mental garden of "What if. . . ?" disaster thoughts during the day as they happened.

Another simple technique that works especially well for the executive-type mind is to think CANCEL. "What if there is a wreck on the freeway and I miss my plane?" Panic in the streets or CANCEL? Concentrate on safe driving, put on Brandenburg's Concerto and the fear thought withers and dies like a pulled weed.

When I first moved to Laguna Beach after my divorce, I worked for three long years at UCI Medical Center in Santa Ana, a commute of about 20 minutes on the freeway. Coming home at the end of the day I turned off the congested freeway to State Highway 133, a winding seven-mile road through peaceful Laguna

Canyon, then owned by the Irvine Ranch and used for cattle raising. My body relaxed, and my mind ceased its computer speed activity to solve the problems presented by the day's activities, including poverty, sickness, death, and internicene political battles for power and turf.

As I gazed at the cows grazing in the meadow or standing under a tree chewing their cud, I thought that our minds are like that, always chewing on whatever we have taken in. If I've taken in good stuff, like the cow that's eaten good grass, when I chew on it again, it digests even more and I'm satisfied. When I've taken in crude, indigestible stuff, I keep chewing on it, hoping to be able to digest it and find an answer.

I'd deliberately think, "Now I'm going home from work to my children who need my love and care, attention and guidance. They need a mother who can give hope, soothe wounds, share victories and defeats, and instruction in delayed gratification. So I must discipline my thoughts, put aside my cares, and attend to the present moment."

How? The first thing I did was to wind down my problem-solving thoughts as I drove through the canyon, soak in its present beauty, whether sunny, foggy, or rainy, breathe deeply, and put on some classical music.

When I got home, my children knew that except for dire emergencies, the first thing I did was take a hot bath. I soaked away the tension and put myself in a receptive mode for mothering and home responsibilities.

Later, as a part of my mental training, I did yoga, Transcendental Meditation (after a year I substituted morning and evening prayer from the Book of Common Prayer), and eventually learned to practice Contemplation. It has been a slow evolution in spiritual practices for a) mental discipline, b) mental feeding, and c) mental cleansing.

My mental discipline must have begun to show because one day a church friend gave me a book with a smile and a twinkle in her eye. "I think you are ready for this." It was titled *Letters from the Scattered Brotherhood,* and I read it every day for several years. It is a collection of essays written before and during WWII by anonymous persons in England, published in a religious weekly, and edited by Mary Strong. The essays are the cumulative wisdom of truth seekers keeping their minds disciplined during extremely troubled times.

With curiosity I began to read and found a fascinating collection of short meditations with an unrelenting prescription for mental discipline leading to purification of thoughts. Just what I needed at the time, it stressed the importance of developing new habits of thinking:

"When hard pressed by old habits and you are under the heavy blanketings of times and events, you, as it were, disappear. This is the moment to step back into the invisible, for there the invisible will enfold you and give you great power in the visible world.

"Acquire new habits. . . ."

"What does your mind feed you. . . ?"

"See your self as a high mountain, calm & lofty, serene and eternal. The daily task, the mean, the malicious, the challenging, the seeming (disaster) see through them all while you are in them, to the lofty pinnacles of your inner self. . . ."

I was challenged to a higher level!

It was true, sometimes in the stress, the busy-ness of a 50-60-hour work week, maintaining a home, and nurturing myself and my two children I lost track of my inner self as my mind raced to solve the myriad of problems.

I needed more than daily doses of positive thoughts; I needed new habits of thinking. How did my parents survive the Great Depression, poverty, loss of family, home, job, and little access to medical care? With faith in God, yes. With emotional support from the extended family, yes. With hard work and hope, yes. But what else, I wondered.

As an adult, I began to reminisce on their mutual thinking processes as shown by their conversation and behavior. My daddy lived in the here and now. On the farm he worked from daylight to dark. He used to say "Man works from sun to sun but woman's work is never done" as an ode to my mother. He worked to make her life easier.

When we went to town to visit relatives nearby we had to be home before dark to feed the chickens and milk the cows. He honored the rhythms of life and nature. He was into problem-solving in the present moment.

My mother was helpless in the face of the depression of the 30s, but she was very good at telling people what to do.

"Cleanliness is next to godliness."

"Tell the truth."

"Do your homework."

She would quote scripture to teach us right from wrong. For instance, "Whatsoever things are good, honest and of good report, *think* on these things."

My sister Joyce wrote a poem for my father's eulogy entitled "I Was His Favorite." Not until she shared it did I know each of us felt the same way. Only she had the perceptiveness to know his gift of making each of us feel special in our own way. You see, my father had the gift of making each of us feel we were the favorite.

I think it is instructive to become aware of both the outward and subliminal messages our parents send us. Then we can evaluate for ourselves what messages are applicable that we can keep and which are like chaff that we can let the wind blow away.

1. Evaluate the situation.
2. Become aware of our response to anxiety.
3. Have hope.
4. Continue mental clearing on a regular basis, just like we need to clean house on a regular basis.
5. Learn problem-solving techniques.
6. Nourish the mind with good thoughts.
7. Practice mental discipline.
8. Become aware of parental injunctions. Sift through them, keep the best, and blow the rest away.
9. Action-Thought

As we clear our bodies, our emotions, and our minds *simulta-neously*, we live to the highest light we have been given *each day*, then more light shall be given.

To keep ourselves in balance, however, we might also keep in mind this saying of Meister Eckhart, a German theologian of the Thirteenth Century:

> "Visible deeds do not increase the goodness of the inner life, whatever their number or dimension; they can never be worth much if the inward process is small or nonexist-ent *and* they can never be of little worth if the motive is pure."

Just as in Chapter One when we talked about consuming healthy food for the nourishment of our bodies, so do we need to consume healthy literature for the nourishment of our minds.

What is healthy literature? Again we turn to the test of time for guidelines for our answer. What literature has endured over time, ennobling the soul, giving food for thought? What books have influenced you the most in your life? If you were banished from civilization for 10 years, what 10 books would you want with you?

Usually, people begin with sacred scripture. The Bible, the Koran. Then the classics: Shakespeare, Benjamin Franklin, and Euripides. Or books of information such as the dictionary or ency-clopedia. I include the poets, especially Longfellow, Blake and Psalms.

As we let go of negative thoughts, false belief systems, and fearful emotions, we need to substitute positive thoughts, truthful sayings and courageous emotions. A collection of truthful thoughts with com-mon denominators of truth from the great religions of the world. Different people resonate to different teachers and traditions.

What authors do you find amusing, enabling, provocative, in-spiring? C.S. Lewis, Madeleine L'Engle, J.R.R. Tolkien, and Piers Anthony are some of my favorites.

As we open our minds we are better able to accept pain and look on the brighter side of life at the same time. We say we have a "perceptual shift." This is best illustrated by answering the question, "Is your cup half full or half empty?"

I was talking to a young man who was separated from his beloved so they could each finish their senior year of college, one on the West Coast, and one on the East Coast. He was miserable, couldn't eat, abandoned good health habits, lived for their phone calls, and couldn't concentrate on his studies.

"I'm trapped," he said. "I want to be with her and I can't." I suggested instead of saying, "I can't" which made him feel boxed in, that he indeed *could* be with her. All he had to do was take a leave of absence from school for a year, live near her and work while she finished her senior year; then she could live near him while *he* finished his senior year.

"You have a choice," I pointed out. "You have both *chosen* to finish school as quickly as possible and then be together."

The light dawned. Able to accept that he had chosen his path rather than being the victim of circumstances, he mobilized his energies, started studying, and used the year fruitfully as a preparation for marriage rather than the helpless victim of circumstances. He then perceived his cup as half full, as he had found the girl he hoped to marry and diligently prepared himself to fulfill that promise.

And finally let us conclude with laughter as a positive mental attitude. Laughter shatters impossible thinking, shatters illusion, gives birth to truth, and above all, keeps us from taking ourselves too seriously. The ability to laugh at our mistakes helps us forgive ourselves and avoid being too critical of self or others. Bill Cosby, the great American comedian, is a living example of laughing at ourselves and loving one another through the occasional idiocy of our ways.

Often I find myself getting so serious, so earnest! Then I see the ridiculousness of my situation and a belly laugh begins from deep inside myself at my utter foolishness!

My spiritual advisor, Father Robert Cornelison (an Episcopal priest), taught me to laugh at myself. One day I called him up, shaking, desperately seeking an appointment. As is inevitable in the course of more than 30 years as a psychotherapist, someone said untrue things about me that were hurtful.

He made an appointment to see me at the end of my day. I walked into his office and with tremulous voice, handed him a fat brown envelope, and said, "I've never seen such a pack of lies in my life!" I was aghast.

He didn't miss a beat.

"Well, of course it's a pack of lies or they wouldn't have a case!" he said.

I stopped, my thoughts stock-still. Then I began to laugh. I laughed so hard the tears ran down my cheeks. At the end of our hour, my whole attitude changed and although there were some unpleasant moments, the deep anxiety and dread were gone. Evaporated. Transformed by healing laughter!

As we begin to clear our emotions of hurt, fear, anger, and guilt, we let go of an emotional load we have been carrying around for a long time. Our hearts are lighter. We get a spring in our step. Our bodies actually feel lighter. As we work through, we let go of past hurts, we "come to ourselves", wake up, and begin to cultivate our spirit. As we break out of the crustations that surround our souls, we find peace we never dreamed was possible.

PART III

Spiritual Discipline

Chapter 5

Sacred Space

As we cleanse the physical and emotional bodies, we can better trust the inner voice and begin to live more in the here and now. As we "lay our heavy burden down", we find ourselves lightening the load in our present life. And we find things around us we no longer need. Parallel to cleaning out our psyche, it is helpful to clear these unneeded items away. Sometimes this is difficult.

I was a child of the Great Depression in the 1930s, and as such learned to hoard wire, wood, dishes, covers, clothes. "You never know when you might need a good piece of baling wire," my dad would say. Simplicity and frugality were appropriate virtues to cultivate after the excesses of the 1920s. But sometimes we carry "putting away something for a rainy day" to the extreme and become a pack rat of useless and unused objects.

A friend of mine recently went up north to visit her parents, long divorced. "It will be easier to visit this time, because they will both be in the same place and I won't have to worry about spending more time with one than the other," she said.

"I thought they were divorced," I responded quite puzzled.

"Oh, they are," she replied. "But there was no more room in the house where my mother lives, so she had to move in with him. That's why he left in the first place. There wasn't room for him in the house anymore." A true story!

Just as we no longer need our anger to protect us or our guilt to punish us, we no longer need many "things" around us. Closets, drawers, bookshelves. Clear, clear, and clear again.

I like books and tend to acquire and keep each one as a treasure. After an accident, lying on the couch for many hours looking up at my full bookcases that line the walls, I realized there were some books I would read again, but others I would probably never read. Better someone else enjoy them, I decided.

Clothes not worn for a year went to the Salvation Army. Bric-a-brac no longer meaningful was given to the church bazaar.

Sometimes we hang onto "things" because they represent people who were or are important to us. I keep my Bird of Peace, Magi, and statuette of Mother and Child because they both have intrinsic beauty and were gifts of love. So is the woven "tapestry" from my daughter's earliest years.

"If there were a fire, what would you take out?" is a question for constructive thought. I'd take my Bible, which was given to me by one of my favorite cousins as a graduation present from high school and the photo album with pictures from my childhood. Although I would miss them, all my other "things" are expendable. Often, as we divest ourselves of "things," we divest ourselves of worries.

As the old spiritual says:

> Gonna lay down my burdens
> Down by the riverside
> Down by the riverside
> Down by the riverside
> Gonna lay down my burdens
> Down by the riverside
> Ain't goin' worry no more.

Like it or not, we do exist in a three-dimensional world of time and space. The living space we create for ourselves tells much about how our minds work, our emotional states and the secrets we hide from ourselves.

My home of almost 24 years is on the market—for sale. I expected to live here the rest of my life and to leave it to my children. But financial considerations, Divine Providence calling an-other direction, and the physical demands of a 61-year-old beach house all conspired in placing the For Sale sign out front.

I've lived there longer than anywhere. It was a rundown fixer-upper when I bought it, and more than 20 years of fixing up let me know it was a perennial, never-ending task. Since my "retire-ment," my calling is writing and teaching rather than puttering in home and garden, and I must move on to simpler quarters.

Although my home is but a rundown beach house, it has charm and warmth and a feeling of peace. When someone comes in for the first time they usually just stand at the door, drinking it in. They, too, feel the warmth, the "make yourself right at home" feeling that the house offers. And if they linger a while, they are apt to fall asleep. In a wingback chair by the fireplace, or on the down sofa in front of the book cases. Or on a worn chaise lounge on the back patio by the pool.

Curiously, if they stay overnight, I get one of two comments:

1. "Your house is so peaceful. I had the best night's sleep ever!"

or

2. "I tossed and turned all night and had bad dreams. This is a spooky house!"

I shrug my shoulders, offer congratulations or condolences as appropriate and remark that others had said the same thing. The house is defined by itself as well as in relationship to its guests.

When we first moved here, I was just out of a divorce, the children were 9 and 12, and two weeks after we moved in I suf-fered a fall and was in bed or in the hospital or at home recovering for 11 months. During this time we lived on a small disability and an even smaller child support check.

For months, most of our meager possessions were still packed in boxes. Our furniture was one step above recycled Salvation Army and I had to sleep on a studio bed in the living room for a year because I couldn't negotiate the stairs to the bedrooms.

During this "twilight zone" of my life, the children not only survived and maintained themselves in school; they were the envy of the friends they brought over. "You must have lots of money," my daughter told me her friend's mother told her. No one else would dare live the way we did. The yard needed a gardener, the house was worn, and pool had neither a filter nor a heater. But the children didn't care. And neither did their friends.

It was a house of love and of healing. They were charmed by the backyard and named it "The Jungle" because it was totally overgrown. They could hide, pretend, and have adventures there.

No one else had a waterbed in the dining room. An octagonal one at that.

And two or three years later, when I spent my last $300 on a pony for my daughter, her friends were *really* convinced we had money. A pony and a pool and a beach house where you could make yourself at home. We had to be rich! We were, but not as they construed it.

I warned the children not to let anyone know we were just short of being paupers as we hung sheets over the windows, used the fireplace for heat, and carried on our "adventure." From these humble beginnings came a mutual support system that held us together. Out of meager belongings and a woefully inadequate budget came a home of peace and refuge from the storms of life.

When we moved in, we agreed "this is God's house" and resolved to take in whoever might need a home—for a day or a week, a season or a few years in some cases. As long as the guests respected the ethos of the house and contributed to its ongoingness, they were welcome. And we all learned with Solomon, "Better a crust of bread in a house of peace than a banquet where strife is."

As anyone who has lived in one place for a long time, I've accumulated more than I need. More than I use on a seasonal basis. And I fall victim to clutter. Sometimes I think the secret of serene surroundings is STORAGE!

The first thing I had built were bookshelves all along the in-side wall in the living room, and above the windows in the master bedroom. I had to have plenty of space for books, rocks, shells, pictures, and favorite things.

One of my idiosyncrasies is that all furniture should be dual purpose. A bed is one of the most useless pieces of furniture around. Why not a captain's bed with storage, a sofa bed for children's and guest bedrooms, bunk beds for space saving? And why so many walls and closed doors? I do believe in respect for privacy, yet there needs to be a flow—a multipurpose house to help us integrate our private selves with our community. Therefore, storage is an inte-gral part of each person's space as well as collective space.

I used to advise poor families with many children to give each child their own cardboard box, available free from the supermar-ket in which to keep their own things, stored under the bed if they had one. Such an arrangement fostered mutual respect and a sense of believing that "I'm an important person."

Coupled with respect for individual belongings, however, comes a respect for community belongings—shared things in shared space to be shared within the family. With guest, with extended family. With mutual respect and honor and responsibil-ity for its care.

My son is excellent at cooking and his cleaning jobs. My daugh-ter at taking care of pets. By cooperating in its function, we all claimed this house as our home. By respecting a Rule of Quiet, each could read, sleep, or follow the beat of their own drummer during those special times. We shared our stories, our own and others' tragedies and victories.

This home, through shared labor, giving to others, and pro-viding inspiration has been our sacred space. And I pray the new owner will feel the warmth, the charm, the ambiance, and con-tinue to honor the house as home.

When I go camping, or to the retreat house, or to a hotel room, my routine is the same, to create my Sacred Space away from home:

1. Check it out, open the doors and windows, clean its very air and atmosphere.
2. Put away all the clutter.
3. Unpack everything in an orderly way, putting things in functional order.

Then I'm ready to settle in. I've sanctified the space and made it mine. It's my refuge, my home, my resting place for a little while.

Then I find a quiet place to be out of doors, if possible. By a stream, a tree, a rock. Once I had reservations at a motel for a conference I was attending. The room I was assigned bore more resemblance to a barroom than a motel room. The carpet reeked with vomit and the bedding of stale smoke. One whiff and I asked the bellman to take my bags to the lobby and informed the desk clerk that the room was NOT acceptable. While waiting four hours for another one, I found a spot of grass in a corner of the courtyard near some bushes and trees, "borrowed" a blanket from another room, and proceeded to set up my "headquarters" there, where I napped, read, and returned to after walks. Finally I was assigned a clean, comfortable room.

Sacred space.

To me, the wilderness is all sacred and must be fought for at all costs. The small plot of land in the mountains of which I am custodian, Table Mountain Ranch, will be left in its natural state as much as possible while I build a home that fits the land. Frank Lloyd Wright said he could never design a house separate from its surroundings—they were an organic whole. And it is our sacred responsibility to create harmony in our external surroundings and to help facilitate harmony within.

My mother, who passes judgment on all such matters, will tell anyone who will listen that it is a crime against nature to build housing tracts or factories on good rich agricultural land, or to despoil the fragile wilderness.

We are stewards, caretakers, of this planet Earth we call home.

So, to create sacred space, we begin with place, geographically. We hallow the land by blessing it and using it to its highest good. Then we build shelter and establish a place for community. And it is our sacred responsibility to create harmony in our external surroundings and to help facilitate harmony within. Sometimes a place becomes imbued with the personalities that live there. Madeleine L'Engle writes of her summer home, "Crosswicks" in rural Connecticut in her book, *The Summer of the Great-Grandmother*:

"It might be said with some justification that all our summers are summers of extremes, because when the larger family gathers together we are a group of opinionated, noisily articulate, varied and variable beings. It is fortunate for us all that "Crosswicks" is a largish, two hundred and some year old farmhouse; even so, when four generations worth of strong-willed people assemble under one roof, the joints of the house seem to creak in an effort to expand."

At my mother's home in Sacramento, I find a sense of what is "proper" in a vague southern way of almost a century ago. We respect mother's privacy and her space, as it reflects the impossible security she so longed for during the Great Depression. The place is "sacred" to her person and we honor it as such.

Sacred. Set apart. Honored. Respected.

I have been in enough retreat houses to know that the house usually reflects the personalities of the Brothers or Sisters who live there. But, no matter how the personalities may rub up against one another creating more friction than light for a moment, there is most always peace in the Chapel. For in the Chapel, most religious and guests put aside their petty bickering, their anxieties and preoccupations, and for a while, attune to a Higher Presence.

Joan Chittister, OSB, who writes eloquently on Benedictine Spirituality in her book, *Wisdom Distilled from the Daily*, discusses the paradox of monastic living. "Monasteries hardly seem like places to go as popular mythology has it, is to leave the world, not to get even more deeply involved with it . . . (but) it may be that those who each have only a bed and books and one closet full of clothes in one small room to call their own who can clearly realize what clutter can do to a life. . . ."

For those of us who choose to live in the great invisible Monastery Without Walls, we need to create a sacred space within our own living places and work places that both reflect our personalities and our commitment to Right Rhythmic Living. That are simple and uncluttered, reflecting a mind that is clear and an attitude that is mindful.

Our Sacred Space is one in which we knit up our own ragged sleeve of care at home, and bind up the wounds of others in our work.

To the naturalist, all of creation is sacred. And all the space between earth and firmament, and deep space beyond. And watery, fiery, space beneath.

My favorite mug carries the inscription:

> "Hurt not the Earth
> Neither the Sea
> Nor the Trees."
>
> —Deuteronomy

And the picture shows a little girl embracing a globe as if it were a favorite kitten.

Such is the attitude we need to foster concerning our earth, our island home. And our domicile, whether permanent or temporary. And our place to draw away a little while to be silent, to be quiet, to be refreshed.

> Hurt not the earth
> Neither the Sea
> Nor the Trees.

The SPACE in Sacred Space. Our living space should comprise as much space as possible in order to allow us to be present in the moment. There are too many "things" in the visible space of most of us.

The idea is to let go of the past and not project into the future. That's how we become "attached" to "things." With simple living space, we are able to clearly communicate what is important in the "eternal present." It does not serve us or our relationships to back track except to correct ourselves, or to hold on to past inflexible attitudes, opinions, or resentments.

I used to visit my great Aunt Emma who was to join her maker within a short time. Everything in her cluttered house was from the past. The fringed lamp shade, the crocheted doily on the chair back. Nothing ever changed, except that there was more of it. Although she was kind, I felt stifled.

Every spring, I go through the ritual of Spring Cleaning. Sorting through, giving away, moving things around.

Let us review seven principles to achieve Sacred Space in our home and healing environments:

1. *Light* Are our quarters light and airy? Is there adequate provision to let in daylight, sunlight every day? Do we have full spectrum lighting if we have electricity?

     Light in the form of sunlight brings vitality to the cellular structure of the body. We are energy beings and light is a necessary energy "food" to sustain us.

2. *Adequate Storage* We need to leave our immediate living space uncluttered so that we are not distracted by extraneous objects and to help us to live in the present. The only way we may achieve this goal, unless we are very poor in world's possessions, is to have adequate storage, neatly organized and labeled. Cardboard boxes, cabinets, storage bins. If something does not hold a useful fruition, pass it on.

3. *Simplicity* To only possess what we need to use, and what is beautiful and has substantial intrinsic value. One person told me that after meditating and seeking guidance she only keeps the clothes she wears regularly, and only keeps in her workspace what she is working on in the present. Saints from Francis of Assisi to Peace Pilgrim extol the virtues of the simple life. A Community that provides guidance to living simply is the Shakers, a 19th century group in America who stressed simplicity in function.

4. *Restful* When entering the Sacred Space is there a sense of peace? Can you rest here? Is the eye caught up in the beauty of simplicity and the excesses of natural surroundings? Is it clean, clear, and functional? Does it serve as an icon to help us enter a more sacred space within ourselves? Does it provide for Sacred Space?

5. *Recycle* In order to keep our living spaces clean, neat, simple, and restful, provisions must be made for recycling the material goods that come, often unbidden, into our lives.

    Nature recycles its creation every season. Can we do less?

7. *Reorganize* Life is dynamic, ever changing. Our lives, our living space needs, our storage space, constant reorganization.

    I love the tradition of Spring Cleaning, with the casting out of what was once so meaningful, leaving room for rearranging the storage, the work place, the furniture. After the dead of winter comes the Spring. Only when we "die" to the attachment to material possessions and recycle them do we leave room for an inpouring of new materials with which to work.

Since our purpose is healing, perhaps we could begin by creating our Sacred Space as a simple perspective from which to heal the world as we create our own monasteries without walls.

Chapter 6

Holy Silence

LET ALL THE WORLD KEEP SILENCE

"In times of momentous occasions
We feel awestruck
We fall dumb; we have no words
We say 'A hush fell over the crowd.'
'You could hear a pin drop, it was so quiet.'
We are moved, yet we have no words,
We are changed by that moment—we are transformed."

When I was 23 years old, I was substitute teaching in an inner-city high school where gangs proliferated and safety was an issue for both teachers and students. My first child was five months old. On the way to 5th period, right after lunch I was intercepted by a student helper with a message to call home immediately. My mouth was suddenly dry, my head hurt, I felt sick.

Without another thought, I headed for the telephone in the teachers' lounge and phoned home. He had a fever of 102 degrees and a cough, and the sitter thought I might like to call the doctor before I came home, as, at four months, he had been in the hospital with croup and was definitely "at risk." I walked in a daze to the classroom, not realizing I was a little late. There was some noise in the classroom as I approached that silenced upon my entrance. I struggled to find my voice. (Later I was told my face was white as a sheet.)

"I—ah," I cleared my throat, but the tears came before the words were uttered. "I'm sorry I'm late . . . my baby is sick."

Trying to breathe deeply, I looked up at the movement at the door. The vice principal (in charge of discipline), the football coach, and another male teacher came tumbling into the room. I blinked with surprise, and they looked startled. Now it was their turn to be speechless. "We . . . ah . . . thought you might need help controlling the class. . . ." the vice principal said. Still tearful, but embarrassed in front of those senior members of the faculty, I just nodded and shrugged, "No."

The class remained silent and still. I waited until they left, then slowly and deliberately walked to the door and closed it, turned to the class and said, "Thank you." By the time I returned to the front of the room I was able to speak, "Now, I'd like to tell you about my baby. . . ." They listened attentively and respectfully. Then I listened to them, about their families, siblings, sick loved ones, their fears. Toward the end of the hour, it occurred to me that I'd better make an assignment, so I asked them to write a paragraph on "When the teacher is late." The essays were astounding. So was the silence as they wrote. Out of my silence came my true feelings. Out of our mutual respect came a flood of words expressing their anguish and pain.

Out of the silence . . . came reconciliation and creativity.

From the heart.

Later, I reflected on the expression, "It was so noisy I couldn't hear myself think." I wondered if that saying also applied to the students. That saying still applies to me.

I don't like noise.

Yet many people create noise, as if they are only comfortable when they drown out any thoughts they might have. They turn on the radio, the stereo, the television. They talk incessantly: they seem oblivious to the cacophony of sounds from automobiles, clocks, mowers, chainsaws trimming trees, electric motors, garbage disposals, telephones, beepers, helicopters and planes. A chainsaw sets my very teeth on edge.

People look at me blankly when I tell them I don't have a garbage disposal because the noise jars my nervous system. (My mother doesn't have a garbage disposal either.) I find all these noises most disconcerting. They disrupt my ability to relax. They interfere with my ability to think and to reflect.

At lunch one day, I went out back to my patio to enjoy the sunshine and the newly blooming spring flowers, especially the intoxicating fresias. In spite of the noise of the automobiles, helicopter and chainsaw, the chirping of robins, sparrows, and mockingbirds warmed my heart. I prayed for the day we no longer depend on petroleum to power our homes, provide our transportation, and foul our air. Noise pollution! Disrupting our health, our psyche, our creative and intuitive processes.

I like to awaken with the hush of the dawn, smile with the first chirp of the birds, pray in the silence and warmth of my bed. Free of pain, free of noise, I enter the silence and *listen!*

Holy Silence.

Like the hush that hangs over the audience awaiting the orchestra conductor to lower her baton.

And I listen to the creaking of the wooden house, as it, too, awakens from its slumber; the squirrels on the roof, the thermostat clicking on, my old-fashioned furnace silently wafting warm air throughout the house, and the wooden house responding with its cracking noises.

And in the silence, I offer myself as a reasonable, living sacrifice to God's work of healing today. Knowing I will be buffeted by storms, by personalities, by fears and real dangers, I offer myself into the keeping of the Source of all life, all love, all creation. I single-mindedly, resolutely accept the price of pain that comes from this offering, knowing I will re-enter the silence with the vesper light, the twilight, the moonlight, the starlight, with *its* silence and be healed by its redemptive, regenerative power.

Margery Kemp wrote in the 13th Century:

"If thou wear the hair shirt, fasting bread and water, and if
thou saidest every day a thousand Pater Nosters, thou
shalt not please Me so well as thou does when thou art in
silence and . . . (Allow) me to speak to thy soul."

I never cease to be amazed at how people punish themselves,
deprive themselves of the necessaries of life and engage in mean-
ingless rituals all with the goal of achieving inner peace or union
with their Creator, or release from anxieties, and feel justified by
their foolish actions, when all they need to do is enter the silence.

Sometimes we need to enter an inward silence in the midst of
outer noise. When this need arises, there is a meditation we can do
even in the midst of the cacophony of noises that surround us that
enables us, for a time, to create an inward silence. This exercise is
no substitute for working to reduce noise pollution, but it does
enable us to enter an island of peace for a few moments. I call it
Sound Meditation. Here's how to enter into it:

1. Sit or lie down in a comfortable position with your eyes closed.
2. Mentally surround yourself with the white light of Christ.
3. Begin to breathe that light slowly, deeply, and completely.
4. Mentally become aware of sound. Just sound. Don't name it
    or think about it, just isolate each sound as it happens—a
    door closing, noises, a truck going by, a phone ringing. As
    soon as another sound occurs, shift your attention to the new
    sound. Without worrying about the exact time, do this for
    about two to three minutes.
5. Shift a little bit and continue the exercise by naming each
    sound as it progressively occurs: Car, bird, phone, etc. Con-
    tinue for two to three minutes.
6. Take a big, deep, breath, stretch, open your eyes, and note the
    relaxation and refreshment you feel.

This five-minute mental exercise you can do most anytime and anyplace and serves as a coping mechanism to deal with noise pollution and still find "Sacred Silence" within, at least temporarily.

Some people like to add a step 6 and just enjoy the quietness to reflect on any problem that may need solving for a few moments before they stretch and resume their regular activities.

I learned this meditation from Norman Shealey, M.D., who is the founder of the American Holistic Medical Association, and have used it in my practice for years. That the mind can screen out unwanted sounds for a time was demonstrated by Milton Erickson, M.D., Ph.D., when he trained himself to sleep where jackhammers were ripping up the concrete. Entering a state of self-hypnosis he told himself the noise was merely that of his own heart beating and thus reassured, he could sleep soundly. William Kroger, M.D., liked to tell the story of how he loved to go fly fishing in the High Sierras. So when anyone started criticizing, haranguing him, he just mentally put himself out in the stream fly-fishing where it was very quiet except for the buzzing of the pesky insects. However, since he had generously applied insect repellent, although he would hear the angry hum of biting flies and mosquitoes, he knew he was protected and could concentrate on his fly-fishing.

Mentally, he entered the Sacred Silence, though he would not call it that, to protect himself from being drawn into defending himself from a personal attack that had no validity and was totally unreasonable.

As a child, I lived in the country, not only with the sounds of wind and rain, cow and pig, but also of oil wells pumping. When we went to town and spent the night with relatives, I couldn't go to sleep. It was too quiet. I missed the pumping of the wells. When the railroad went from steam to diesel, we lost the long, low, mournful whistle. The conversation of the adults centered for some months on the meaning of the omen associated with the loss of that whistle. For most, it was the beginning of the downfall of civilization as we knew it, the end of an era where individuality counted and the trains ran on time.

The same argument ran for electric clocks. "If you can't hear a clock tick, how do you know it's running?

Clock winding was a nightly ritual that for some of us soon became associated with winding up the universe so the sun would come up the next morning. "All I could hear was the clock ticking," someone would say. And the others would nod in agreement. What they really meant was that a near catastrophe had been arrested because the clock still ticked! Just like my heart still beat.

In Oklahoma, we had tornadoes and lightning storms. We children had to jump into our metal-framed bed without touching any metal, and stay between the feather beds for insulation. Sometimes we could see electricity dancing on the bedposts. It was exciting and exhilarating!

But the story that impressed me the most (and kept me safely between the feather beds), was the story of Aunt Jewel's Clock. Seems that lightning hit it, melted one leg, knocked it clean across the room—yet it still ticked on time.

Yes, ticking clocks were very powerful to me as a child. A powerful fetish to keep the world turning and the sun coming up.

Even today, I have century-old wind-up mantel clock above my fireplace, a German box clock in the office, and a French wall clock in the bedroom. By focusing on the tick-tock, all the other sounds ebb out of consciousness and I enter Sacred Silence.

Sacred Silence is *active*. As one of the Letters writes (p. 137):

> "Be *active* in silence
> Strong in peace
> Keep thy strength in gentleness
> Rest with the Song of gentleness about thee
> Fill the inner reaches with love
> Bathe in Spirit
> For it is sweetness to thy bones, flesh and health.
> Keep in holy (silence) and listening, OBEY."

During the silence, we can attune to the yearnings of our heart and out of our entering into the Sacred Silence comes strength, peace, and health.

Such is the paradox of the strength and power of the receptive silence. Obedience to the inner voice that comes from the silence must always be tempered with wisdom of the heart.

We have all heard and read of tragedies that have occurred from the acts of the "true believer" who follows an inner voice to extinction!

A young man I knew very well swallowed poison because he "heard" the voice of Billy Graham tell him to swallow poison or he would be tortured. I learned this as I sat with him in the emergency room after his stomach had been pumped and tried to explain that Billy Graham would never tell him to do that.

Another time he jumped in front of an oncoming truck because "The Devil told me I could fly." It was a miracle he survived. But he stopped heeding the destructive instruction of voices after that.

Before we "obey," we need to talk to our mentor, to exercise restraint, to use discernment. Edward Sellnor writes in his book, *Mentoring,* that the true voice from the silence is hesitant, not insistent, and one should go through much soul searching before acting upon its promptings. "Perhaps the call itself is never recognized as decisively or as clearly as it seems to be by those who later write of their discovery. What many of us have in common is what many call an 'Inner Voice,' or an emerging inner conviction . . . The inner conviction is eventually perceived as the voice of God, a moment of grace, contact with the sacred, the call of life to our souls . . . Our response is usually ambivalence or reluctance. . . ."

With such discernment, comes a commitment to help others. Out of the silence is the birth of our calling. As we mature on our journey into healership, into loving service, we can also enter the sacred silence to contact our mentors.

We begin the process of mentoring with just being together, with sharing and caring. As we become more comfortable with one another, we meditate together silently; thus learning to transcend time and space. Eventually, the student can contact the mentor in that Sacred Silence though the mentor is not physically present.

Chaim Potok tells such a story in *The Book of Lights*, speaking through the experience of a young rabbinical student who studies both the Talmud, the book of laws, and the mystical tradition, Kaballah, which teaches that time and space are transcended in relationships of teacher and student. The young student Gershon Loran is ordained a rabbi and goes to Korea to serve as a Chaplain during that War of the late 1940's. There he builds a little hut, called a succah, in which he can pray and also, through meditation, contact his teachers, Nathan and Jakob. The advice they offer is reasonable, practical, and encouraging, such as "Take care of yourself, you are looking quite thin." Or they tease a bit to lighten his load.

"It is a big succah, Loran. You had in mind the seminary succah when you drew up the plans?"

"The camouflage effect is intriguing."

"I think we will study a little, and then leave. What do you say, Jakob?"

"A little Talmud cannot hurt."

"Not nearly as much as a little Kabbalah."

"What shall we study, Nathan?"

(Potok, Chaim, *The Book of Lights*, N.Y. Fawcett Crest, 1981.)

Gershon sat very still in his vision and studied the Torah with his two teachers . . . guests in the *silent* interior or his succah on this cool Korean night.

The Inner Voice is practical, or a "Practical Mysticism", as Evelyn Underhill would say.

Sellnor also believes that people of wisdom from the past, relatives we love who have passed on, as well as present-day teachers can be with us in sacred silence. Usually in a place designated for that purpose, sometimes called a succah, poustinia, cell, or inner room. Wherever we find silence and solitude.

Although I was used to silence from living in the country without electricity for the first 9 years of my life, and in seeking solace in nature throughout the rest of my life, the silence of the monastery was an entirely different experience.

Twenty-eight of us ate supper together in silence in the communal dining room at Mt. Calvary Retreat House in Santa Barbara where the only sounds were the clinking of cutlery, the nervous clearing of throats, and the scraping of chairs. It was an unnerving experience.

Where do I look other than my plate? How do I ask for the salt? How do I say excuse me when I inadvertently elbow the person in the next chair, or drop my napkin? When I get tickled over an absurdity, may I laugh? Or worse yet, how about when I get the giggles? After dinner in the general meeting in the Common Room, one of the monks explained about the silence.

"Here we respect the integrity of each person. It is considered an intrusion to interrupt another's thoughts and reverie. Therefore it is polite to remain silent on meeting someone and rude to speak under ordinary circumstances." Out of this ethic, we were taught to become aware of our speech, our laughter, the sounds of footsteps, doors closing, even laughter. Noise is an intrusion.

When my husband and I had a small motor boat shortly after we were married, one of the rules of the sea was, "You are responsible for your own wake." For the waves produced by our boat in passing another could cause damage.

In the same way, at the Retreat House, I learned to be responsible for my own sounds, spoken and otherwise. The Great Silence would start at 10:00 p.m., after which conversation was permitted only in an emergency.

At first I found the silence in the presence of others to be oppressing. Solitary silence I could enjoy, but this group silence was unnerving. I was so used to relating to other people that it took time and self-discipline to gradually draw inward sufficiently to find quiet, sacred space, sacred silence.

After I found the quiet center core of myself, only then could

I relate on a totally different level to my companions—a kind of quiet acceptance, respect and knowing. An intimacy without intrusion, without becoming a pleaser. After a few years, I became so accustomed to the inward serenity that I felt in the silence that I resented any intrusion. And I began to feel more at home with the silence of the heart so well expressed in the old hymn, "Near to the Heart of God":

> There is a place of quiet rest,
> Near to the heart of God;
> A place where sin cannot molest,
> Near to the heart of God.
> Oh Jesus, blest Redeemer,
> Sent from the heart of God,
> Hold us, who wait before Thee,
> Near to the Heart of God.

With the withdrawal into sacred silence I then became more aware, sometimes excruciatingly aware, of my fellows than I ever could, or had in the presence of words.

I began to look forward to those "silent" weekends with certain members of my parish. We called one another "my retreat buddies" and, though we knew little of our regular daily lives, we cared intimately and communicated at a deep level that I can only describe as the soul level. This led me to the following conclusion: "Until you have been on a silent retreat of at least three days with someone, you do not know them."

Hence, another paradox:

Entering into the silence, withdrawing into the sanctuary of our inner being, is not an antisocial act. In fact, its effect is the opposite: After being in silence with someone for two or three days, when we do talk, we converse about meaningful things, true emotions; we bare our souls and drink from the milk of human kindness.

From my experience with silence in the monastic community

came an awareness I can write about but only the experience can make it real for you. There is a saying in psychology "What is your frame of reference?" In the colloquial we would say "Where are you coming from?"

One of the goals of psychotherapy, according to Carl Rogers, is to help a person change their frame of reference so as to be more cogent with their own best self. In Shamanistic vocabulary, this process is know as "changing your assemblage point." Or "Here's how I see it from where I sit." Implicit in the statement is "Change the place you sit and you will see the situation differently."

A Native American expression saying something similar is "Until you walk in another's moccasins, do not judge."

Applying this knowledge about perceptual set to the changes we experience in Sacred Silence, I can say "Unless you enter the sacred silence, you cannot begin to enter the necessary inward presence necessary to channel God's healing energy. And, of course, the converse is also true. As you learn to enter the interior silence, you develop the *presence* necessary to bring the healing to the situation you are in. You are *both* more personally removed and more intimately aware of the person or situation to which you wish to bring healing. You are *both* more aware and less personally involved. It is an exquisite paradox of pouring oneself out in order to be filled.

Learning to keep silence in a loving intuitive way can also be utilized to enhance relationships.

When I first invited one friend to go on retreat with me at Mt. Calvary Retreat House, she balked when I told her about keeping the silence. She saw nothing sacred about it. She'd had 20 years of pain associated with a frozen silence her spouse turned on her when he was angry. He wouldn't speak for days—then at some unpredictable time would erupt in a violent temper.

No words of mine could convince *her* that silence could be healing. So on our first trip I arranged the time where there would be a "talking weekend." Keeping silent from 10:00 p.m. to 8:00 a.m. wasn't so hard for her. In fact she began to appreciate the quiet. And so, the next time we went, she was able to enter the Silence from 8:00 p.m. Friday to 8:00 a.m. Sunday. I also promised she could talk to me at any time she got panicky.

Actually she did pretty well, and I saw her out in the garden assisting the monk gardener in charge with a smile on her face. It was only after she *experienced* the healing power of Sacred Silence that she could articulate fully the pain of "separation silence." And learned to appreciate the difference.

When I used to counsel couples sometimes I became convinced that the only reason for their arguments was it was the only time they expressed real emotion. And, just as children would rather be punished than *totally* ignored, so do some couples argue as the only way they know to achieve closeness . . . such as it is. In these cases, I began to teach substitution of other methods for arguing. Such as going to movies, theatre, and other spectator events, or working side by side in home or garden without words. Or having a silent meal by candlelight, fire light, twilight.

To enter the silence and learn to be silent to enhance intimacy went a long, long way toward helping the relationships to grow in trust and togetherness. About the same time I was learning to enjoy the silence on retreat, my young teenaged children went away to an Episcopal church camp.

My daughter, the storyteller in the family, was recounting her tales of camp life suddenly stopped, her eyes grew wide, she smiled and exclaimed:

"And guess what! You aren't going to believe this! Oh, we thought it was going to be so weird! But on our last day there, we had a Silent Breakfast! And it was so neat! It was like a contest to see who could keep from talking and our tent won first place. We were really proud of ourselves."

Sacred Silence is a vehicle for changing interpersonal relationships as well as for personal growth.

Enjoy!

Chapter 7

Holy Leisure

In Chapter 1 we talked about the rhythm of our lives and recalled the lovely lilting music from Fiddler on the Roof:

> "Sunrise, sunset
> Sunrise, sunset
> Gently go the years."

The same kind of rhythm takes place between the busyness of our lives and our leisure time. Holy leisure is that take it easy, down time when we are not working or doing anything purposeful that, *in the balance of the rest of our lives*, makes us whole. Whole. Of one piece. Holy Leisure. That balances us between "busyness" and "rest." All or nothing at all.

When I first began making retreats to Mt. Calvary Retreat House in Santa Barbara, I'd take a full briefcase of work to be done or books to read, or I'd plan my time. Saturday morning I'll get up early and hike to the stream before breakfast, I'd tell myself. Then I'd find that I slept in instead. I thought my intentions were good, but somehow I never got around to doing what I planned.

At first it was sleep that interfered. Although I got up without an alarm at home, here I invariably slept in. And when I lay down to read my book, I'd wake up an hour or two later. Morning and afternoon. I barely made it to meals!

Or, somehow, I'd get distracted. There always seemed to be a more interesting book in *their* library than the one that I'd brought.

Or more interesting people to talk to than I met at home. Somehow I'd meet someone more alive, more creative, more focused— just plain more interesting. They defied classification.

A monk who was clairvoyant; a retired priest who had gone into primitive lands, invented an alphabet and given the people a written language; a Franciscan nun on leave from the Near East, being on retreat with monks to study art. A burned out inner-city nun who wore street clothes and sang with the voice of an angel; a Dominican nun who taught me liberation theology for women and predicted a woman pope by the end of the century! A Baptist preacher who did yoga every day and genuinely worried about the low percentage of men in churches; the college student who came to study, the artist to paint, the movie star to seek seclusion. The anthropologist, the emergency room physician, the nurse.

We came, we slept, we ate, we worshipped and took long walks, watched spectacular sunsets, and laughed and wondered. Now, when someone asks me what I do when I go on a retreat, I say, "I just BE." And that's what Holy Leisure is: a state of beingness, alone or with others that, although planned for, has no plan. Though wished for, has no particular end product.

When I was growing up, Saturday was Clean the House Day and Sunday was Sabbath, rest day. Well, I must confess to being caught scrunched in a corner of the hall reading the encyclopedias rather than dusting them, most of the time. To lying on the bed watching the patterns of sunlight on the ceiling rather than making it up; to searching for four-leaf clovers rather than mowing the lawn.

But I did learn certain valuable things. For instance, we could never wash the bedding and then put those sheets directly back on the bed. We had to take the clean ones out of the cupboard. Why? Because the fibers were stressed from the laundering process and had to REST.

"Actually," my mother told me, "One should have three pairs of sheets for each bed, because the sheets were much happier and lasted longer when they were able to rest two weeks instead of one." Made sense to me!

The story is told of a wise teacher who took an overly enthusiastic young monk out to the woods for target practice with his bow and arrow, for the young monk was a hunter. "Take an arrow and shoot it as far as you can."

Immediately on striking its target the monk commanded he take another arrow and repeat the process. And another. And another. And another. Until the young man finally said, "Good Sir, I pray thee, I must stop."

"Tired already, surrah?" inquired the teacher with a twinkle in his eye.

"Oh, no sir, but my bow is stressed and certainly must rest or surely it will break."

"Ah, and so will you, my dear young fellow, if you do not learn to pace yourself. Are the fibers of your bow that much dissimilar to the fibers of your body?"

Chagrined, the young monk began to learn to pace himself, and no longer fought against his time for Holy Leisure.

As a teenager, I burned the candle at both ends whenever I could get away with it. I loved the excitement and the stimulation of activity and socialization.

About this time I read the autobiography of Tallulah Bankhead, the famous actress with the sultry voice who closed her book with the verse about the candle that she burned at both ends:

"But oh my foes

And oh my friends

It makes a lovely light."

It took several bouts of physical exhaustion for me to learn that I could *not* burn my candle at both ends, and that no light was lovely enough to make up for the darkness that followed.

Holy Leisure.

I may read a book, take a nap, go for a walk, have dinner with friends, but the purpose of what I do is not the accomplishment of that task or act, but what that activity does for me in the whole picture of my life to bring me back into balance and harmony with myself. Afterwards I smile more, I feel content.

Many years ago, a young friend asked if I'd ever gone on a vacation by myself. Now, where would a single woman go, I mused. Well, the more I thought about it, the more attractive the adventure became. "Oh, you've got to go to Victoria, British Columbia," he said, "It's so civilized." Refinement appealed to me but once again the old question, "But what do I do?"

Undaunted, he plunged right on. "Well, first you've got to stay at the Old English Inn. It's full of antiques and the food is authentically British. Then let each day develop by itself." And so I did.

I decided I'd have dinner every night at the hotel as a home base, and made a reservation every night for 6:00 p.m. Whatever I did during the day, I was home, showered and dressed for dinner by 6:00. The waiters and waitresses became my good friends and a good audience to hear of my day's exciting adventures.

I snuck into Parliament with a touring high school class, had tea with a real English Lady at the Empress Hotel, whom I met by chance, got lost driving my rental car on logging roads, was thoroughly frightened at the Wax Museum by decapitated heads from the French Revolution, and thoroughly delighted with the truffles the inn served for dessert.

Besides having a whole week of Holy Leisure, away from schedules, deadlines, and pleasing others, I also had little times during the day of just plain goofing off. Staying in one foggy day and reading my book, or walking on the wharf. Now I'm finding I need down time every day. To randomly water and weed my flowers, to watch the sunset, to walk on the beach.

Holy Leisure is not watching television or spectator sports.

That is recreation, diversion. In Holy Leisure, we let our minds wander off wherever they will; the actions of our bodies, such as walking, are automatic, and take no particular thought.

A good English word that may describe what I do in Holy Leisure is "putter."

When I was a child, I used to whittle. At first it was twigs, and later, when we moved to town, popsicle sticks.

Anyone who asked, "What are you making?" obviously didn't understand whittling. When you whittle, you whittle for its own sake.

Or fishing. Especially without a hook.

As children, we really wondered about adults who kept saying when we asked if we could go to the stream, "Well, what are you going to do there?"

"Well, just hang out!"

"You'll get into trouble!"

Oh, adults!

"I think I'll go chop wood" can be used for Holy Leisure if a person needs to get off by herself to get some physical exercise and let the mind rest a while.

So can reading. I remember the writer, Madeleine L'Engle, saying at one of her spiritual retreats not to plan activities. "Read a good book. Maybe a detective story or murder mystery." "*Get out of the way* and let God do the healing work."

Oh my, I thought, surely I should be reading something religious or inspiring. But as time went on I came to know the wisdom of her words. And I learned to get out of the way and let God do the healing work.

Whatever is meant by the scripture on the creation, where it is written "And on the seventh day, God rested . . . And looked over all he had created . . . and behold it was very good"? What we have here is a model for reflection, for evaluation, for self-affirmation for our creative endeavors.

Show me an artist who is busy all the time and I'll show you a star that is burning out.

Rest, reflection, affirmation.

This weekend, my daughter, a friend and I plan to drive to Idyllwild, California, for a weekend of doing just that. "Idyll in the Wild." We have reservations for a rustic but secluded cabin. Our agenda is to follow our own rhythms, visit a few friends, walk in the wilderness. Forty-eight wonderful hours to sleep, to laugh, to experience nature, to go up on the mountaintop and get a perspective on our life below. Evaluate our lives honestly and make changes to bring ourselves more into the wholeness of our being within the divine creation. Will we be able to say, "And it was very good"?

> Rest, reflection, affirmation.
> I can affirm what's good in my life and like chaff, blow the
>   rest away.
> Holy Leisure.
> Sounds of Silence.
> Purposeless, purposeful activity.
> Maybe we'll take a picnic lunch to the stream or to the lake.
> Or plan where to build our mountain cabin someday.
> Maybe the outline of a new book will come to me in a full
>   blown inspiration that I'll jot down in my notebook.
> Maybe I'll collect rocks.
> Maybe I'll browse through some quaint shops.
> Maybe we'll go out for Chinese food, or Scandinavian, or
>   fish.
> Maybe. . . .
> I'll rest when I'm tired until I'm rested.
> I'll walk into the forest until I'm chilly.
> I remember as a young teenager really liking to sing the
>   Country Western ballad "Don't Fence Me In":
> "Oh give me land, lotsa land
> Under starry skies above—
> Don't fence me in!
> Let me ride by myself in the country

That I love
Don't fence me in!
Let me be by myself in the evening breeze
Listen to the murmur of the cottonwood trees
Send me off forever but I ask you please
DON'T FENCE ME IN!"

Freedom! Of activity—of thought—of purpose.
Freedom—to be.
Freedom!

That's Holy Leisure.

I hope I have not misled you into equating any specific activity with Holy Leisure.

A gambler playing pool for money or prestige is not engaging in Holy Leisure. My nephew playing pool on Friday night after a week of teaching junior high school is.

My daughter going trail riding on her favorite horse is engaging in Holy Leisure; her friend competing in the arena is not.

On a rainy day, sitting pensive in front of a roaring fire, pen in hand, vaguely melancholy, watching words shape themselves into a poem under my hand is Holy Leisure. This afternoon, focused on trying to communicate a concept as foreign to our culture as Holy Leisure, is NOT.

A friend of mine came to visit. She was very unhappy in her work. Surprisingly she was doing what she thought she had always wanted to do. She had bought an old barn in New England, fixed it up to live in the loft, and sell homemade crafts in the store below on weekends. The barn was her studio. Her artistic creations, which she used to delight in making were still in demand and were acclaimed and appreciated. She made an adequate living.

"But I'm not happy," she said. "All I do is work. I've got to restructure my life so that my art work is for me—I used to enjoy creating. Friends wanted to buy what I had to offer and soon I was taking orders and commissions. Somewhere along the way I lost

my creative self! I'm thinking of taking up quilting for a hobby—
and never selling a one!"

Another friend makes miniatures and presented me one day
with a miniature of an adobe house, Santa Fe, circa 1955. It hangs
on my wall in a place of great esteem. So far he has resisted all
offers to sell his miniatures. "First," he says, "I could never get
enough for them to pay for my time; and second, I don't want to
risk losing the joy I get from doing them." He knows that should
the motive change from poetry to profit, he would lose his Holy
Leisure, his inward self.

Holy Leisure.

Do you get lost in time? I do. Does Time stand still, go slowly,
rapidly, or exist at all? For me, Holy Leisure is Kairos, God's time,
while work, generally, is Chronos, clock time or sun time.

Do I have a feeling of equanimity, of serenity, of satisfaction, of
refreshment afterward? Do I have a hard time remembering what I
was angry, upset, or anxious about before? Do I see my life, my
work, my faith in more perspective? Do I feel quiet and peaceful
inside?

Then I've successfully experienced Holy Leisure.

I am more whole.

Chapter 8

Sacred Sex

What is the place of sexual expression in the life style of the healer?

To come from the heart, as in everything else that one does. Yes, including sexuality.

The question is not necessarily with whom or when or how. The questions are:

Does sexual expression in this way at this time with this person come from the heart?

Is it an act of love? Is it truly a heartfelt expression?

Is it within a committed relationship of sexual fidelity between adults who understand the consequences of their action?

Have any previous relationships been resolved and loose ends gathered up?

Is there pureness of heart in both parties?

Does the physical expression have a spiritual basis (Love the Lord thy God with all thy heart, mind and strength and thy neighbor as thyself)?

Is there a commitment to helping one another in good times and bad, to grow and mature in wisdom, to forgive and go on?

Is there deep and genuine caring?

Does the physical expression of sexuality lead to an enhancement of one's spiritual qualities of healing, truth, beauty, integrity, courage, and compassion?

Does the physical act open the heart wider, balance the energetic field, and enhance healing potentials?

These are some of the questions we ask as we consider the role of sacred sex in the life of a healer.

Sacred Sex for Healers and Teachers

Healers and teachers become aware of dimensions of energy and reality beyond their five senses of touch, taste, smell, sight, and sound, beyond the three dimensional planes of height, depth, and width, beyond that which we call the physical, beyond time and space, beyond our local selves.

Our great love songs bear witness to the "beyondness" of sexual expression in new found love:

> "Some enchanted evening
> You may see a stranger
> You may see a stranger
> Across a crowded room. . . .
> And somehow you'll know. . . ."

There is a sense of recognition, of knowing.

Three dimensional words are inadequate to describe the experience of heart felt love. Elizabeth Barrett Browning wrote in her immortal love poem to her husband Robert,

> "How do I love thee? Let me count the ways.
> I love thee to the depth and breadth and height
> My soul can reach, when feeling out of sight
> For the ends of Being and ideal Grace.
> I love thee to the level of every day's
> Most quiet need, by sun and candlelight.
> I love thee freely, as men strive for right;
> I love thee purely, as they turn from Praise.
> I love thee with the passion put to use
> In my old griefs, and with my childhood's faith.
> I love thee with a love I seemed to lose

With my lost saints,—I love thee with the breath,
Smiles, tears, of all my life!—and, if God choose,
I shall but love thee better after death."

Beyond the three-dimensional universe of time and space, our souls unite in a love that both includes and transcends the human body. The paradox is that physical love is an expression of soul love that includes and goes *beyond*, transcends the physical. Or expands the physical "through all eternity."

Eternity is not seen as chronological time extended forever like a spider's web flung into space. Eternity is encompassing every dimension of our own existence—expanding simultaneous universes exploding with love.

"I love thee now, I love thee now
And through all eternity."

Madeleine L'Engle has portrayed simultaneous realities in her book, *The Swiftly Tilting Planet*, in which words of power proclaimed with intention and courage save the planet earth from the demagogue's destructive search for ultimate power:

"In this fateful hour. . . ."

The powers of this love over the powers of destruction are absolute.

Lovers stand suspended between the forces of creation and destruction of one another, themselves, and their relationships.

When love comes from the heart, the relationship can grow and flower and bear fruits of the spirit to all it touches. When lovers get caught up in power and possessiveness, they are subject not only to the destruction of their own relationship but to their health and healing work. In physical expressions of heartfelt love we are becoming co-creators with the universal force I call God.

Examples can be taken from our speech.

We enter into the "spirit" of the occasion.

We "celebrate" Christmas, birthdays, anniversaries, the Eucharist.

These words are symbols of something deeper, something beyond our local selves.

In the Hebrew faith, God told his people in the Ten Commandments, "Thou shalt have no graven images" to an invisible God. Only a container for the Ten Commandments called an Ark. An Ark of the Covenant between God and humankind that gave rules of living with the promise that as one obeyed these rules, God would dwell within that person and bring a sense of unity with the co-creative process. The human heart now serves as an Ark, a container, a covenant between Spirit and flesh. "Thou shalt have no graven images."

Graven images, gods of Baal, of a male bull expressing sexual energy with no energy of love—raw animal interest without any redemptive, transforming nature. A graven image is a sacrifice of the "other" for one's own pleasure rather than sacrifice of the "local self" for the beloved which brings compassion, kindness, and great joy.

In our initiation process toward healership, we slowly become aware of energies beyond our three-dimensional world. Various great religions throughout history have provided words, rituals, and theoretical concepts to describe the various ways of perceiving energies that are beyond physical perception, yet are present as an act of love. Of loving kindness toward our fellows. (Charles Tart in his book, *Transpersonal Psychologies*, has succinctly described these various world religions within a psychological context and the reader is referred to this classic work for a historical knowledge of these great world religions within their common universal core of unity.)

Understanding the precepts of the Ten Commandments and the law of love as expressed by Jesus Christ as the incarnation of love is a necessary part of becoming a healer.

As healers become more aware of the spiritual nature or underpinnings of physical manifestations they begin to understand the mystery of incarnation, "of the Word made flesh."

The mystery of incarnation is that the material world proceeds in an orderly fashion from the spiritual world, and that we do not as yet have an understanding of the process of how this takes place.

As the healer proceeds through the initiation process of complete obedience to the law of love, and the thought and emotions are purged or purified of impediments to heart-centered being and living, there comes a softening and a strengthening of the human personality.

Celibacy

For some, the unity of the healing process involves a life of celibacy where union with the spiritual dimension is sufficient to all things. For some of these it is because there is a supremacy, a fulfillment that comes in solitariness that is beyond sexual expression. That is sufficient.

For others, celibacy is a necessary purification process of the physical nature when it has been allowed to overextend itself and block avenues of spiritual growth. This happens when jealousy, strife, domestic violence, lust, selfishness, murder, or rape have been a part of one's past. Better to choose celibacy until such a time when there is a definite spiritual calling to another path. These choose the celibate path, whether for a time or a lifetime. (I personally believe vows of celibacy are best taken yearly, for who can predict the path of spiritual growth?)

For the healer, no sex is better than non-sacred sex. Non-sacred sex does violence to ourselves and to those with whom we partner. It contributes to shutting down a part of ourselves, therefore contributing to the compartmentalizing or cutting off of a part of ourselves rather than to committing to the wholeness necessary to healing.

Celibacy by Circumstance

There are several reasons for times of celibacy. The first we might term circumstances. One may be celibate simply because of circumstances. There is no one in our known circle of acquaintances with whom we feel drawn to in the circle of the sacred fire of sexual expression. Examples:

1. One is asked, "Are you dating anymore?" and responds, "No, I'd rather be alone than go out with someone who's only interested in sex as (choose one): a one-night stand; for dessert; without commitment."
2. A young man going off to war took a vow of celibacy as he didn't want to risk disease or father a child in a time of stress.
3. After a long and happy marriage, one partner dies. The surviving partner feels no need or desire to unite sexually with another. This is particularly true of women who have satisfying relationships with extended family.
4. "Why aren't you married?" "I've just not found anyone I wish to be married to."

Celibacy by Choice

Although there is some overlapping of these two categories, in celibacy by circumstance we primarily mean there is no one available who is a potential partner for the sexual expression of heartfelt love in a committed relationship.

In celibacy by choice we shift the focus to the deliberate choice regardless of availability or desire.

Examples:

1. One who joins a religious order with the intention of loving God and serving humanity without the constraints of partner or offspring.
2. One who has been deeply hurt in a relationship and needs time to heal.

3. One who has hurt others in violent ways and forswears a relationship as a time of cleansing and penance. One that can't quite trust oneself to enter into relationships until certain emotions of possessiveness, jealousy, potential for violence, or lust have been purified through abstinence.
4. One who has been the victim of aggression or hurt, (i.e., #3) and needs time to heal.
5. One who feels called by God to be celibate for a season or a lifetime in order to achieve a higher purpose.

In a relationship, but especially a sexual relationship, there is the potential for the misuse of power. When one is coming from a power position rather than a loving position, both are hurt.

The master teacher, Paul of Tarsus, wrote that we are not to be unequally yoked one to another. I take that to mean no sexual relationships are possible between adult and child, between employer and employee, between therapist and client, between teacher and student, or doctor and patient. When a sexual relationship begins to grow, unequal power position through roles should be eliminated or ameliorated.

In heart-centered love, there is equality, freedom, and commitment to the well-being of the other. "Love thy neighbor as thyself."

It is a servant relationship to one another: "How may I help *you* become your own best self?"

When there is inequality because of power, celibacy is the rule until and unless the possibility of abuse is eliminated. Even then, it is very difficult. An officer resigns his commission, or the enlisted person gives up the service. The patient chooses another doctor, the client another therapist or attorney, the student another teacher, etc. When there is wealth, steps are taken to correct the balance of power so that even if the relationship ends, the other is provided for in basic needs of food, clothing, shelter, and medical care. (Some men treat their mistresses better than their wives in this respect.) How many wives stay with their husbands because they don't know how they would survive in the world (especially when there are dependent children) without the financial support of a spouse?

What Sacred Sex Is Not

Sacred sex is not a plaything, though it may be very playful.

Sacred sex may not be used as power over another, though sacred sex may empower both.

Heart-Centered Love and the Creative Process

Heart-centered love knows no bounds of age, gender, race, or class. Once a person is physically mature, expressions of heart-centered love in sacred sex lead very naturally and very quickly to a committed relationship, excluding all others as long as the love is alive (as opposed to, "As long as both shall live!")

The marriage ceremony, or the private vows might then read, "I take thee to be my spouse, to live under God's holy laws of love, in good times and bad, in sickness and health, so long as our love is pure."

Purity of love is purity in heart.

Purity of heart leads to right actions.

Right actions are also defined by a spiritual interpretation of the Ten Commandments, by social traditions of respect and civility and honor and courage, of standing fast in adversity, in the glory of human sacrifice for another as stated in the scripture: "Greater love hath no one than this, that he lay down his life for his friend."

Courage. Sacrifice. Freely given love will be expressed in living and through sacred sex.

A teacher/healer who cannot live these principles of purity of heart had best remain celibate.

For human sexuality correctly expressed becomes an awareness of joining in a creative way the energies of creation. Sexual energies, properly shared, become an adjunct to healing energies. Let's not get the cart before the horse. First comes a joining of the souls united in God's purposes of bringing healing to the relationships, of a genuine desire to pour out one's self in service to God, to ones' fellow human.

One definition of sin is separation from God's love.

This transcending love finds two souls drawn to one another. As they share words, thoughts, common endeavors, as they begin to feel "one" in spiritual ways, they may then be drawn to one another physically.

In the course of human events, as the mental, emotional, and spiritual selves unite, their physical selves then seek expression of the already common experiences, feelings and thoughts in sacred sex.

Sexual joining that expresses the sacred nature of the unity between the two beings, their commitment to serve one another and their commitment to heal themselves, one another, and others.

One same sex Christian couple I knew, after taking vows to one another of fidelity and caring, tenderly washed one another's feet in the symbol of service to one another.

The ceremony of foot washing that Christ himself instituted on the night of the Last Supper (Passover) before his crucifixion was utilized as the symbol of humility and service that his followers were to give to others.

Some have said, and rightly so, that sacred sex is an act of procreation, to have children. And this is good. But to limit sacred sex to the procreation of children is to limit the creative act. God's creation story did more than bring human beings into existence! There is also art, culture, music, law, drama, horticulture, architecture, and sculpture, among other things.

When a couple gives sexual expression to their heart-centered love, this energy propels them to even more creative ways of service to others.

One couple I know recovering from previous hurtful marriages, both with grown children, affluent in material goods, in taking

their marriage vows also established church membership in a congregation that had a mission to the homeless, the disenfranchised.

In their maturity they had already established their homes
and their children were "out of the nest." They were also aware of
the preciousness of their own love, and that they must continue to
give beyond themselves. So they joined together with a community that provided homes for the homeless—people that they never
met—but they felt were part of God's unusual family.

Others adopt orphans, take in children from shelters or off the
street, support orphanages, shelters for battered women, and other
good works. They are expanding the energies enhanced by their
sexual union into works of healing as co-creators with God.

Privacy

Sacred sex is a very private experience.

Jesus said, "Go into your closet, your inner chamber, to pray."
This may be interpreted as literally going into a private, quiet
room as Agnes Sanford suggests in her book, *The Healing Light*,
and it can also mean going deep within ourselves to the silence of
our sacred space to better attune to the still small voice of God.

Similarly, lovers go into their own sacred space to make love.
Sacred sex is private. Only in privacy can true lovers look into one
another's eyes and commune soul to soul, heart to heart, and achieve
a depth of caring and devotion that then is expressed passion to
passion.

Laughter, delight, healing; coming together in private enables
the couple to go forth, together or separately, to serve others more
lovingly.

In sacred sex there is a molding, a blending of the energies.
My essence becomes that of my beloved as we bring together our
souls and bodies.

Talking is an important part of lovemaking. Processing and
storing mentally throughout.

Tears provide release of past hurts. As I am held, sustained, as

I share my hurt, I am able to leave behind old hurts and am filled by Christ's love through my lover, to let go the fear and heal with love.

Empathic abilities are enhanced and grow exponentially with the intimacy of sacred sex.

Lovemaking is the goal, not achieving a climax. Passion waxes and wanes. When it wanes, this is a time to talk, to sleep, or to lie quietly until something emerges to share. Sacred sex transports us to realms beyond our local selves to a dimension which is holy. We feel united with the infinite.

During lovemaking one is opened to perceptions, knowledge, insight, compassion, the oneness of creation, and the desire to help and heal others. To be part of an expanding circle of love.

Yet the lovers remain cloistered, private, almost secretive. Their love is sacred, almost too sacred to speak about. Like the name of God, JHV could not be spoken. For such a great love cannot be reduced to words alone without being lowered to the mundane.

And so it is spoken in poem, in song, in ordinary living so that each kindness becomes an act of love.

After time has been allowed for the private expression of sacred sex, the lovers are not separate even when separated geographically. There is a telepathic link, an empathic link.

One couple I know, even though separated, "knows" when the other is awake and can't sleep. The second president of the United States, John Adams, and his wife Abigail, corresponded every day. Their letters show they were "together" though separated by distance for long periods of time. Another couple, separated for a year, "felt the presence of the other sleeping together every night . . . I go to you." Usually a couple knows about an infidelity. "I just sense it."

Is distance an artifact of perception? Studies of the blind whose sight was restored reveal people not being able to comprehend spacial relationships. Many adults could not learn to live in a three-dimensional world once their sight was restored. Researchers found then that space perception is a construction of a person's mind.

The Sacredness of Lovemaking

The Song of Solomon is the most overlooked book in the Bible in my experience. Sanctimonious or prudish preachers dismiss it with, "It is a metaphor of Christ and the Church," or the relationship between the soul and God. Those statements may indeed be true.

But I see it as more. As bringing the divine fire into the physical act of lovemaking as sacred sex.

The poetry of the book of the Song of Solomon is its first clue. Poetry by definition transcends linear thinking and opens us to the Song of the Soul beyond time and space as we understand it.

> How fair is thy love, my spouse
> How much better is thy love than wine!
> And the smell of thine ointments than all spices.
> Thy lips, oh my spouse, drop as the honey comb.
> Honey and milk are under thy tongue,
> And the smell of thy garments is like the smell of [the cedars
>   of] Lebanon.
> A garden enclosed is my sister, my spouse,
> A spring shut up, a mountain sealed.
>
> Song of Solomon 4:10-12

> I am come into my garden, my sister, my spouse.
> I have gathered my myrrh with my spice.
> I have eaten my honeycomb with milk.
> I have drunk my wine with my milk:
> Eat, O friends; drink, yea drink abundantly, O Beloved.
> I sleep, but my heart waketh. It is the voice of my beloved
>   that knocketh, saying, "Open to me my sister, my love,
>   my dove, my undefiled, for my head is filled with dew,
>   and my locks with the drops of the night."
>
> Song of Solomon 5:1-2

The marriage is between our sexuality (root energy center)

and our spirituality (crown energy center). Between speaking the truth in love, and our emotional selves (throat and solar plexus). Between our mind, intuition and intellect, and our ego (brow and belly). So we meet in our heart.

And heart reaches out to heart loving and healing. A channel for God's enduring love.

And so we end as we began.

Physical lovemaking is a manifestation of spiritual love. As we surrender ourselves to God's unconditional love in complete obedience to living the law of love, we offer ourselves, our souls, and our bodies as a reasonable, living sacrifice to God.

> As we open to receive,
> So do we give,
> Becoming a stream of clear running water,
> A channel for God's healing love.

> "For lo, the winter is past, the rain is over and gone,
> The flowers appear upon the earth,
> The time of the singing of the birds is come
> And the voice of the turtle dove is heard in the land."
> Song of Solomon 2:11-12

> "And there abideth these three things, faith, hope, and love,
> but the greatest of these is love."
> I Corinthians, 13:13

Chapter 9

Commitment to Right Rythmic Living

There have always been healers and communities of healing. Mostly passed on by communities based on religious tradition. Through advanced communication, we can learn the principles of Right Rhythmic Living, and anyone who wishes may follow these teachings. The growth of the spiritual self evolves through many paths. Think of a candle-lighting ceremony. One candle is lit; the flame is passed on, one by one, until the cathedral glows in a soft incandescent light, the light of truth. So may we learn to ignite the spark of God within, one by one by one, and pass it on to each one we contact through our own beingness and creative endeavors.

Those who have been fortunate enough to have met personally with Mother Teresa said they were forever touched by the experience. That she radiates with a kind of glow. That their lives are softened and illumed. That they become more loving.

I don't understand how it happens, but I believe that it happens. William James in his classic book, *Varieties of Religious Experiences* (1908) wrote eloquently of lives changed by hearts being touched by the Infinite. I live my life according to that belief, that touching the Infinite opens our hearts to healing.

As I make the COMMITMENT to participate in my own healing and perhaps follow the path of the healer, I am making a COMMITMENT to love. To accepting love whether I deserve it or not. And to live the path of love whether I believe the other person deserves it or not. And that path includes, inevitably, pain. Just as it is painful to go through emotional clearing, so there is pain involved in the path of COMMITMENT to living a life of love. But somehow it's bearable. Even rewarding. At least it is for me! As the older boy replied when the man asked if he weren't tired of carrying the younger boy a great distance upon his back, "He's not heavy, mister. He's my brother."

Why is pain necessary? We are shaped by forces from above and we are shaped by forces from below. The conflict between love and fear, love and selfishness create tension which creates pain but also leads to growth.

Living in the now, within the circle of love, provides the balance and eventually meaning, even in pain. The form of the circle is a symbol for holographic thinking. The circle is love, joy, and a sense of protection. A COMMITMENT to healing is a COMMITMENT to feeling. To feel we must have a COMMITMENT to be in the physical, to be connected to that experience in the physical, knowing it will bring with it some pain. The pain becomes the teacher. The pain and suffering, the fears we feel will pass as we align ourselves with the circle of Infinite love and return that love to "the Earth and all that is therein."

Some people fear to love because they fear the pain. When we truly love, the pain is bearable. In dealing with pain and fear, we learn to go to our hearts and go beyond the pain by aligning with our COMMITMENT to love. Sometimes I could only get through the day by saying "My mother loves me and God loves me no matter what, and I will find my way."

By continuing to commit myself to loving service in spite of the physical pain, I found guidance and a sense of protection.

One of the country-western hymns of my childhood was "Will the Circle Be Unbroken?"

Essentially the song is asking, "Is our love for one another spiritual enough to transcend physical and ego limitations?" The circle representing first of all our family of origin, then our family of procreation, our family of friends, and eventually, the family of humankind and the universe even beyond the planet Earth.

I was fortunate enough to find an old tape of country-western music during one of my lowest times, and the tears brought forth a release not only of worry and tension but also an affirmation in the invisible hand of love that joins me to all the lives that have touched mine—the sea of eternity of our caring for one another.

Loving is a serious COMMITMENT. It involves staying conscious, staying present to be with the feelings in the present. Slowly we find peace as we release the pain, the anger, and the fear.

It is a daily task!

Sometimes, I get so impatient with my body for not being able to keep up with my mind! I have a whole book in my mind just waiting to be written! That's when I need to remember that what is needed at the time is necessary. The process of healing takes time.

I accept the inevitable delay, I return to rest. Then busy-ness distracts me. When I become aware of the distraction I return to the circle of Infinite love, to my COMMITMENT to Right Rhythmic Living. I walk, I eat, I drink water, I visit with friends, I laugh, I rest my body, I allow time for intimacy, I return to the work.

Compassion for self precedes compassion for others. Pain teaches me compassion for myself. Compassion teaches forgiveness of myself. Forgiveness leads to love for myself. Love diminishes my pain and fear and leads to healing mind and body. As I'm patient with myself, I find myself being more patient with others.

I found I was causing more pain than need be by thinking that I absolutely knew that's how things were supposed to be. The more I let go of my pre-conceived ideas of how I should be, or how others should be, I could be more gentle with myself and others.

"Let there be peace on earth, and let it begin with me" goes the folk song. Only then can we move to our task of healing.

> "To balance the earth with love,
> To cast light where shadows linger,
> Moving darkness into light,
> As night yields into day.
> In rhythm with ourselves,

We are healed in the process,
By our focused intention to love,
Beginning with ourselves.
Then there will be,
Peace in our song,
Joy in our heart,
Love in our ways."

As we continue to follow our COMMITMENT to healing our bodies the discomfort will subside. Working thru the pain we may feel as if light has permeated our entire body. We continue to clear away the congestion in our physical and emotional selves. Then the light of our soul pours into our minds, enabling us to solve problems as they occur.

One person, after having meditated as was taught in Chapter Two with the Lake Meditation, reported her experience (there were many more to come) of clearing like this:

"As I was listening quietly to the tape, I experienced tears and relief. I was sitting up and simply listening to the words. I was aware of light trance, but alert, like when I'm writing on the computer. I listened to the tape again, and this time felt my whole body clear as if the light had entered and wiped it clean inside. I noticed a dramatic clarity when I stood up. A lightness throughout. There was no pain or discomfort. I was feeling hungry, so I had some food, a baked chicken breast, which also felt clear in my body."

This was the first of many healings in order to build the structure and foundation of what was to come for her. She experienced more pain as she began to clear her emotional hurts. When she had a temporary lapse of her COMMITMENT to Right Rhythmic Living, she felt lost.

There are times, of course, when rules and regulations block the path to enlightenment. It is then appropriate to devote time and energy to changing those rules. These are trials to accompany the light of the soul! I've learned to bless the situation, work through my fear and pain, and let the discomfort of the conflict pass into a belief that there is a Higher Justice, a higher more noble purpose. No small task!!

Growth proceeds in a progressive way as a daily experience with its ebb and flow, ups and downs. As we grow, we experience disruption. As we release our lives into God's guidance, we address issues of obedience, discipline, detachment, loneliness, self-responsibility, and self care. It is a path of surrender to the work God has "called" us to do.

As we go along, there are times in keeping our COMMITMENT when we are afraid to go forward. Two psychological concepts are helpful to me in understanding when to go forward and when to take a step back. These are: l) Regression in the service of the ego and 2) Acting out.

Regression in the service of the ego is going back to a time where we were more comfortable. It's also covered by the old expression "Sometimes retreat is the better part of valor."

The right action for "regression in the service of the ego" can be sleeping on a problem, a purchase, or a dilemma before taking action; going fishing at the end of a busy time; taking a vacation before starting a new job, or popping popcorn and watching an old movie after a difficult day.

Acting out is going back to a time when we were hurt or persecuted and acting in such a way that we get ourselves hurt or persecuted again—violated, nagged, judged, criticized, raped, or beat up. We behave in such a way to either cause ourselves to be the victim or misconstrue others' actions to feel we are being victimized.

The boy or girl who was molested by their grandfather (next door neighbor, pastor, teacher, aunt) as an adult might become a prostitute or a whore, stay in a loveless marriage or engage in seductive, destructive liaisons.

The child who was not protected may become the parent who either neglects or over-protects. One father I counseled, who was battered as a child, deliberately chose a position as a traveling sales representative knowing he couldn't cope with being a 24- hour father. But he was an excellent and devoted part-time father. After two years of therapy, he took a position in a supportive community that involved only occasional travel.

The child who was abandoned may either smother by devoting oneself to their progeny, or abandon, or criticize others profusely for what they perceive as abandonment on the part of others such as another parent who travels or works outside of the home.

Once a man came to me for therapy because he had struck his wife. He had never hit her before. She had provoked him by capriciously canceling a mutually planned vacation, embarrassing him at work and when confronted, pushing him and taunting repeatedly "Hit me!" He did not condone his own behavior and concluded they both needed counseling. Both needed to make changes which, slowly and painfully, they did. They learned to live in the present more and "act out" less. And they both learned to take "time-outs."

Regression in the service of the ego gives us breathing room to fall back, rest, regroup, consolidate our forces, and go forward wisely. Acting out always leads to more pain and the perpetuation of the problem that caused the fear in the first place.

Letting Go

As the tasks and demands in our lives increase, the path of COMMITMENT becomes more difficult to follow. It is seemingly easier to submit to a path of one's own choosing than, by faith, to follow our evolving perception of God's will. The closer to the present we can remain, the easier it becomes. "I can deal with today, it's next month I can't handle," most of us say.

The other day, faced with whether to pay the rent or the taxes from the present inadequate cash flow, I took a deep breath, told myself the taxes could wait and reminded myself I had a home, a car, food to eat, and clothes to wear. I had been in this situation before and all bills eventually got paid. Of course, it was also an opportunity to look at my lifestyle and to assess it for simplicity.

Anxiety about tomorrow? Try this. Pay attention to NOW. Within the word NOW is the circle. Go inside the circle of love and expand the present moment. To experience an immediate relaxation and release in the physical body, center yourself, breathe deeply.

Listen to your body. When you haven't been listening to your physical body for an extended period of time, you lose your grounding. I know. It happened to me. Without a solid attachment to grounding to both present reality and faith in a beneficient Presence my vitality was depleted, anxiety ran rampant, and I got out of rhythm with myself. That's how I "fell victim" to Epstein-Barr.

Importance of Commitment

Groundedness is another lesson in the COMMITMENT to leading a disciplined life. Many people follow a discipline for a while, doing what they know they should do, and then fall back into old destructive habits or life patterns for one reason or another. Usually setting unrealistic goals or expecting immediate results.

It is the discipline of the repetition of the right behavior even when we grow weary that is necessary. Some people rebel with repetition. I know I don't even like to follow the same recipe twice. We rationalize and rebel. Then we persevere in our rebellion to "prove" it doesn't matter, closing ourselves off to adjusting our course.

The secret is realizing that the repetition of right behavior provides the structure for innovation (freedom) within the rest of our lives, freeing us to be creative and alive and well! It is by going deep within, breathing deeply, and allowing the initial discomfort of repetition to pass that we succeed in remaining on the path to health and truth.

Many fail at the start and elect to stay on the surface of life with froth, pleasure seeking for pleasure's sake, diversion and escape. Through suffering or boredom, they may finally wake up, see the light and begin to pursue the more difficult but infinitely more rewarding path to trust and enlightenment. The sooner we surrender to this truth the quicker comes the satisfaction of a life well-lived.

Remember the old proverb of the straight and narrow?

Straight is the path and narrow is the way that leads to life. Broad is the path and wide is the gate that leads to destruction.

It is truly our choice at each given moment.

Let's talk a bit more about the necessity for grounding in order to learn to trust our intuitive selves. We know that our electrical equipment must be grounded; well, so must the healer/teacher.

Sometimes as we desire to evolve into the best we can be, we attempt to do so without the necessary anchor of common sense. Then we get over-excited about some new teacher/ healer/theory/ method and "lose ourselves," our good judgement, our "horse-sense " as my Daddy would say, and get carried away on a wave of emotion. Without the discipline of Right Rhythmic Living, it's easy to make fools of ourselves. I've done that.

When we become over emotional we are at risk of getting caught up in group hysteria. My teacher Dr. Pullias, Dean of Pepperdine College, used to remind us to "beware the mob." In my senior year in college some of the men's dorm decided to have a panty raid on the women's dorm after hours. (Unfortunately, I slept through the whole thing.) The next day at chapel, Dr. Pullias frowned on what most of us considered a harmless episode. He did not object to the panty raid, per se, he objected to group (mob) consciousness.

"Why did the fellas make the decision to raid?" Because fraternities at other schools were doing it and a few guys wanted to be "one of the boys." Group inclusiveness is used to frequent houses of prostitution, to gang-bang (serial rape of one girl), or to join a lynch mob or the KKK.

When "to belong" is the motivation, a person will tend to abandon his own principles and engage in behavior he would otherwise judge to be ludicrous or reprehensible.

When we are well-grounded in ourselves we are less likely to engage in behavior that is of a mob-consciousness, self destructive, or hurtful to others.

Committment to Physical Clearing

Physical clues to ungroundedness are to notice where we put our feet, how we stand, how we experience the awareness of weight in our bodies; and where our focus of awareness is concerning our body parts. Phyllis Greenacre, who wrote the classic *Psychosomatic Medicine* (1946), shows how mind and body are connected and interact upon one another. A personal assessment process may give us clues as to where the blocks of energy flow are located. Blocked energy prevents the life stream from entering or exiting the body— thus weakening the life force. Many body workers, such as Alexander, Lowen, and Feldenkrais have evolved techniques for releasing bound up energy.

The dissipation of the vital force is slight at first and usually goes undetected, but as time goes on and there is an inevitable challenge to the body in terms of stress of any kind and symptoms begin to appear such as ulcers, colitis, or headache. Ultimately perhaps hypertension, cardio-vascular disease or cancer.

The first lesson in healership is connecting to one's innate common sense, then connecting to nature. Getting one's own life stream to flow uninterruptedly first, and then flow continuously with more vigorous force before any energetic exchange occurs is vital for both healee and healer. This creates the appropriate anchor for boosting the life stream. Basically, we have to clean up our own act before we can expect to have energy left over to help others.

Some people experience earth as mother, as nurturer, as life itself. As we extend the duration of our daily walk, we begin to become aware of our powerful connection to earth as Creator.

Simplicity

Good healers are often seen as simple people without complexities of lifestyle who live a life unburdened by "things."

Living in simplicity is a state of high evolvement. The healer has discovered that instead of expending time and energy on items of useless intrinsic value (often encountered in the materialistic world) that a simple lifestyle enhances enjoyment of living. Living in simplicity is an ancient truth for peace of mind that we all need to cultivate.

Let me give you an image of simplicity and the importance of the earth. Accept the image as a metaphor. Let's imagine ourselves living in a community of like-minded persons out in nature. We are walking along with a friend in an open field. Our house is made from stones found on the land. We feel at peace. Holding to a simple image such as this may help us move away from those things that deplete and distract us from our life-work as we heal ourselves.

Our desire to pursue the life-work we are called to do becomes stronger than any other internal drive. Frustration arises from outer influences and pressures as well as from within. One solution is to simplify. I do not mean to imply hardship or deprivation such as my mother had to suffer on the farm during the Depression. Clearing out our living area gives us the space to resonate within and around us.

From the time I was a teenager our family camped out every year at Yosemite National Park. We pitched our borrowed tent at Camp 12 where the stables were and where the church of Christ Family Encampment was located. Between two streams and across from a wilderness meadow, this yearly sojourn became my "trip to Mecca."

After my divorce and on my own with two children to raise I wanted to continue the tradition of camping out. Because the valley was now flooded with tourists I naturally ascended to the High Country, sparsely populated, quiet, and primitive. I taught my children how to pitch a tent, build and douse a fire, cook over a campfire, chase away bears, and spend a whole day watching the insects around the campsite prepare for winter, or silently wait to watch marmots or squirrels at play. Or catch a fish with a hook on string tied to a pole.

One summer we decided to go without ice or cooler and ate dried food or used the stream as our refrigerator. We reveled in the simple life and came back refreshed, rejuvenated, literally joyous with our discoveries and coping ability.

"Give me the simple life."

As we let go of the items that are no longer needed in our lives, we become aware of how they encumber and impede our growth. We let go of material things as well as old feelings and thoughts that are associated with them. As we heal our emotional and mental selves, along with our physical bodies, a sense of lightness replaces a certain sense of being burdened and our hearts begin to sing.

Magnetic purity is the key to our work and that is achieved through living the Right Rhythmic Living pattern, beginning with groundedness and simplicity.

As modern life progresses, we are to use the tools of technology to enhance our work so we live the lifestyle that is supportive of ourselves and our work.

Fly the airplanes, use the computer, drive our cars, work for reimbursement, and receive the riches coming to us. And steal away to the wilderness for refreshment.

May God bless you richly as you live out "The Song of Your Soul."

Chapter 10

This Is My Song

Not long ago, my friend Jose remarked at a group discussion one evening as he was telling his story. "I am seeking my song. The song of my soul."

His comment set me to thinking: What was *my* song, the song that expressed my innermost longings and purpose?

I began to review my musical heritage, the music in my head, searching for my heartfelt yearning, "The song of *my* soul."

We sang at home and in family gatherings around the piano or pump organ when I was little. This was in the days before television, and I miss it. But "the melody lingers on."

My sister Elaine remembers from her earliest childhood days our father coming into the room after work and singing as he did a soft shoe shuffle,

"...."

And she would respond,

"...."

And when my brother was born, Daddy would rock him to sleep at night while singing the Plain song:

> "My little baby is a boy.
> He wears a little white suit,
> He goes to church and Sunday school,
> And seems to like it, too."

So, I grew up thinking it was normal to think in terms of music, of rhythm, and song.

When I was nine, our family began to attend the Church of Christ where the whole congregation sang a capella. Everyone participated. We "resonated" with one another. It was a glorious time.

But what was *my* song? Where was I coming from? How do I find my song?

The songs to which I resonate are mostly folk songs—at least the tunes are, because these melodies speak to the heart. They run around in my head unbidden.

In the Prologue I quoted:

> "This is my story
> This is my song"

The words are from the chorus of this early-American hymn with words by Fanny Crosby, a blind woman who nevertheless found great peace in surrendering her life to her Lord. The music by Mrs. Joseph Knapp is like a plainsong or folk song, very easy to sing and to remember.

When I first learned of the blindness of Fanny Crosby I was aghast. Not yet 12 years old, to me blindness was the worst possible thing that could happen to someone. I was both repulsed and attracted to the blind people that walked haltingly down the street, tapping their white canes.

The song of praise, of calm and assurance from a poor old blind woman added a new dimension to my budding theology— that one could find peace in suffering through faith in God was astounding.

Happy or blessed?

Filled with goodness and love?

That paradox remained an unsolved mystery for many years as I came back to it again and again. But I didn't reject the song itself as I understand many hymnal editors did. "Too sentimental, too simplistic" they said.

Their comments were even more incredulous to me than the words of the song. Simplistic? A blind woman finding peace in suffering? Who do they think they are kidding?

Fanny Crosby told her story, and I am enriched in its telling.

Later the words of the chorus took on a new meaning as I realized the importance of each one of us telling our story. For over 40 years in my work as a psychotherapist I have listened to people's stories with attention and understanding.

And now, I tell my story and share my song of what it is for me to be a Christian with the hope that the courage to tell my story encourages you to tell of your own spiritual journey, from blindness to "visions of rapture."

When I was in the fourth grade and attending a small Church of Christ with my parents, it was the custom each Sunday to have an invitation hymn where we were invited to come forward and make the statement that we were committing (or recommitting) our lives to Christ.

This was the first year we lived in Sacramento and the first time in my life I had attended a church regularly. I found the Bible study fun, because I already knew more than anyone there (except Bill Chase, whose mother had also taught him at home) and I loved to excel. I was beginning to take the idea of conversion very seriously.

Although I had never known a time when I didn't believe in God (God as loving Creator, the Spirit that gave life to all things) it was a child's simple acceptance of the way things were. But, in fourth grade, while walking home from Tahoe Grammar School with Rose Minasian, I was looking up at the clouds, white, fluffy, and filled with light after a recent rain.

And I said to myself, *I* didn't create those clouds. No *person* made those clouds. So who did? After giving the matter a great deal of thought and my undivided attention for at least two or three minutes that spanned an eternity, I reached the only logical conclusion possible. Since humans were the smartest creatures that existed, and since they didn't make the clouds, then there had to be a Higher Creative Intelligence.

That concept I called God. (And I've never doubted since).

Well, then I began to take seriously the preacher's words that it wasn't enough to have a private belief, but it was necessary to proclaim and act upon it as well. And that follow-through started with having the courage to walk down the aisle to the front of the church, to answer the question, "Do you believe that Jesus Christ is the Son of God?" With a "yes" right out loud, and then to be baptized as a symbol that I was starting life anew by accepting Christ as my guide and constant companion through life.

As a part of that conversion experience I was to inwardly grapple with my sins, confess them to God, say I was sorry, and resolve to live a changed life with God's help.

Well, I knew I had sins. I had a stubborn streak, a willfulness to do it my way, and sometimes I was "sassy" (rude to my parents).

And I stole. I stole an eraser from the five and dime in the third grade and felt the excitement and the delicious feeling of getting away with it and the pride of its possession and the shame of it all.

So, when the invitation hymn began, tears began streaming down my face. I was so sorry! And I knew that I wanted to run down that aisle and say yes! Even though at that time I was so shy that I though I might pass out if I had to stand up in front of everyone.

Here is the song that expressed my total surrender to God's love for me at the time:

> Just as I am! without one plea,
> But that Thy blood was shed for me,
> And that Thou bidd'st me come to Thee,
> O Lamb of God, I come! I come!
>
> Just as I am! and waiting not
> To rid my soul of one dark blot,

To Thee, whose blood can cleanse each spot,
O Lamb of God, I come! I come!

Just as I am! tho' tossed about
With many a conflict, many a doubt;
With fears within, and foes without,
O Lamb of God, I come! I come!

Just as I am, poor, wretched, blind,
Sight, riches, healing of the mind,
Yea, all I need, in Thee to find,
O Lamb of God, I come! I come!

Just as I am! Thou wilt receive,
Wilt welcome, pardon, cleanse, relieve;
Because Thy promise I believe,
O Lamb of God, I come! I come!

Just as I am, Thy love unknown
Has broken ev'-ry barrier down;
Now to be Thine, yea, Thine alone,
O Lamb of God, I come! I come! Amen.
—Words by Charlotte Elliott, 1836

And at that moment, nine years old, every word of that hymn touched my heart and I responded with my whole being. I knew I belonged to God, and I was ready to act upon it. But my parents constrained me. I wasn't old enough, they said. I didn't know what I was doing. I had to wait until I was older.

They were physically stronger, so I didn't get to go forward. But I added both a sin and an understanding with God to my soul that day.

One, I hated my parents for not understanding. And, second, God and I knew my resolve, and I would never be dependent on another person for my relationship to God again.

There was a built in rift between me and any other human being who tried to define God or my response to God for me. Oh, I was hungry to be taught and still consider myself a student. But I have my own private relationship, thank you, and I'll express my confession and my Christian life out of the relationship and inner conversion I made that day.

Because my commitment carried with it the process of forgiveness I was forced to confront my hatred of my parents for restraining me. As I grew into adolescence they became alarmed when I didn't go forward to be baptized. Not me. No siree, Bob! Somehow I was given the opportunity for a private confession of faith and baptism so the deed was done. But it took me years to forgive this lack of understanding, though I wasn't very proud of my former hatred now evolved to resentment. But finally, this verse got to me and I entered into mystery of forgiveness. They truly didn't know any better.

> "Just as I am, thy love unknown
> Has broken every barrier down
> Now to be Thine, yea, thine alone,
> O Lamb of God, I come! I come!"

"Blest be the Tie": Another Song of My Soul

As an adolescent I was a fervent Christian and loved going to church. I loved the music, the people, the answers to philosophical questions and the pot luck suppers. I attended every service, Sunday morning, Sunday night, and even Wednesday night prayer meeting. (Though I could never figure out why they called it a "prayer meeting" since it was really Bible study. Mostly I asked embarrassing questions. The one that stands out most vividly was "What is a holy kiss?")

I guess nobody ever asked that question because I got some weird answers. At any rate, the evening was all new, enjoyable, and at the end we sang a hymn, had a prayer, and went home.

We were told to sing a hymn because the Bible said, "And they sang a hymn and went out."

My favorite hymn at parting was "Blest Be the Tie that Binds (our Hearts in Christian Love)." These people loved me and I loved them and was truly pained to leave them until the next service.

Now, I teach the song to my retreatants. For me, living in community, the third verse tells it all:

> "We share our mutual woes
> Our mutual burdens bear
> And often for each other flows
> The sympathizing tears."

"Amazing Grace": Another Song of My Soul

Amazing Grace brings tears to my eyes every time I sing it. I don't remember the first time I heard it, though I do have early memories of its tune. The words I didn't understand for a long time. It has been said that more Americans know and love this old hymn than any other sacred song; and can sing it. It has the lilt of a lullaby and a message of hope.

The most moving rendition I've ever experienced has been the a capella version by Joan Baez in live concert, when she asks the audience to join her.

> "Amazing Grace, how sweet the sound
> That saved a wretch like me.
> I once was lost, but now I'm found;
> Was blind, but now I see."

When I watched the television documentary on PBS by Bill Moyers on tracing its beginnings, I was profoundly impressed by its account of the conversion of its author. A former captain of a slave ship, he truly repented of his ways and became a Scottish Clergyman, writing many hymns. The music is simply listed as

"Early American Melody," yet it does not bear any likeness to any other song of its type. Upon musical analysis, historically it bears the most resemblance to early Negro Spirituals whose tunes were often brought by the slaves from their native homeland. Should this hypothesis be true, the implications are "amazing": the most embraced sacred song of our land—combining the words of a repentant slave trader with the melody of the slaves with their unquenchable human spirit.

There are some people who object to the word "wretch" in the second line,

"Amazing Grace, how sweet the sound
That saved a wretch like me."

And there are some hymnals that have "cleaned up" these lyrics. I find these laundering efforts an effrontery to the human spirit.

Who among us, certainly not I, can say we have lived a life never having done something that we feel "wretched" about. Whether in blind ignorance, out of fear or deliberately. I certainly have done things I have later regretted deeply and cried bitter tears over when I "came to myself." I prayed, "Oh God, forgive me!" for I was beyond human forgiveness of anyone I knew.

And who of us can say we have survived danger, toil, and fear solely on our own merits? For my part, I have survived, endured, grown, and prospered by God's grace.

"Dear Lord and Father of Mankind": Another Song of My Soul

In college, I made a lot of mistakes that later I felt very foolish about. For many years afterward, the song I resonated the most to was taken from the poem by John Greenleaf Whittier, which began:

"Dear Lord and Father of mankind,
Forgive our foolish ways!
Reclothe us in our rightful mind,
In purer lives thy service find,
In deeper reverence, praise.

Ode to Joy: Another Song of My Soul

Beethoven's 9th Symphony, Hymn of the Universe, is to me one of the most glorious, ennobling hymns ever written. A friend of mine who died of AIDS recounted before he died that the most glorious experience of his entire life was singing Beethoven's "Ode to Joy" in the original German in concert in Berlin. He lived life fully, from the carnal to the spiritual.

Though his early training was Episcopalian, he was truly a man of all seasons and no church or creed could contain his brilliantly creative mind, his loving spirit, his biologically caused mood swings from deep depression to pinnacles of ecstasy. He was honest, caring and quite impossible to live with. I loved him, and knowing him has enriched my life. Experiencing this song through his eyes has deepened my appreciation for the transcendence of the human spirit.

I want Ode to Joy sung at my funeral. Richard and I will sing along with angels from the other side.

"Joyful, joyful, we adore thee,
God of glory, Lord of love;
Hearts unfold like flowers before thee,
Praising thee, their sun above.
Melt the clouds of sin and sadness;
Drive the dark of doubt away;
Giver of immortal gladness,
Fill us with the light of day.

THE Song of My Soul

As I really searched for the song of my soul, however, I began to realize more and more that what I related to most was a calling to relate to things in a spiritual way and to give service from this calling. I never really felt like I "belonged" anywhere except my grandfather's house, Pepperdine College, Laguna Beach, California, Yosemite National Park, and the land in the mountains above Palm Springs where I hope to build a retreat house.

And those places were temporal, ever-changing. I began to see the common thread that ran through my life was indeed to follow the beat of my own drummer and, wherever I was, to live up to the highest standards of loving service of which I was capable.

And so, the song of my soul became, "I Am a Stranger."

> "I am a stranger here
> Within a foreign land
> My home is over there
> Beyond a golden strand.
> Ambassador-to-be
> To lands beyond the Sea,
> I'm here on business for my king.
>
> This is the message
> That I bring
> The message Angels
> Fain would sing.
> Oh, be ye reconciled
> Thus says my Lord and King
> Oh, be ye reconciled to God."
>
> "I am a stranger here. . . ."
> "Oh, be ye reconciled. . . ."

Reconciliation. Not in a smooth it all over sense, but in a coming to grips with the basic issues sense. Yes, my family taught me that.

At times there is a dissonance. Life is like that. But after the discord comes the resolution. Like in music, reconciliation of a discordant chord.

For me, reconciling my basic self with my best self, reconciling my self to the Creative Essence from whence I come became the Song of My Soul.

What is the song of your soul?

Epilogue

"Words are the language of the intellect; music is the
language of the soul. When you speak from your intellect,
you make words. When you speak from your soul you
make music."

- Elaine Deatherage

We are teachers and healers, passing on to each person we
touch a bit of our own essence—our being, our beliefs and attitudes.

Whether or not we're aware of it, we also pass along our story
and our song.

I've told my story,
I've shared my song.

What is YOUR story?
What is YOUR song?

Suggested Reading

Angelou, Maya. *The Heart of a Woman*. Bantam, New York: 1997,1981.

-----. *Wouldn't Take Nothing for my Journey Now*. Wheeler, Hingham, MA: 1993.

The Book of Common Prayer. The Church Hymnal Corp., New York: 1979.

Braly, J., M.D., *Dr. Braly's Optimum Health Programs*. Times Books (Random House): 1985.

Great Songs of the Church. Abilene Bookstore, Abilene Christian College, Abilene, TX.

Vickery, M.D., and Fries, M.D. *Take Care of Yourself*. HMO Colorado, Blue Advantage.

James, William. *The Varieties of Religious Experience*. Penguin, New York: 1982.

L'Engle, Madeleine. *Troubling a Star*. Farrar, Straus, and Girroux, New York: 1994.

-----. *A Wrinkle in Time*. G.K. Hall, Thorndike, ME: 1998.

-----. *The Crosswicks Journal*. Harper and Row, New York: 1972.

-----. *A Ring of Endless Light*. Farrar, Straus, and Girroux, New York: 1980.

Longfellow, Henry. *Poems*. Houghton Mifflin, New York: 1882.

Meissner, William. *Ignatius of Loyola.* Yale University Press, New Haven: 1992.

Norris, Kathleen. *The Cloister Walk.* Riverhead Books, New York: 1996.

Sanford, Agnes. *The Healing Light.* Macalester Park Pub., St. Paul, MN: 1947.
-----. *Healing Gifts of the Spirit.*

Schafer, D., M.D. *Relieving Pain: A Basic Hypnotherapeutic Approach.* Jason Aronson, Inc., Northvale, NJ: 1997.

Shealy, N., M.D. *Ninety Days to Self-Health.* Dial Press, New York: 1997.

Sinetar, Marsha. *Ordinary People as Monks and Mystics: Lifestyles for Self-Discovery.* Paulist Press, New York: 1986.

Storr, Anthony. *Feet of Clay: Saints, Sinners, and Madmen: A Study of Gurus.* Free Press, New York: 1996.

Watkins, J. and H. *Ego States: Theory and Therapy.* Norton: 1997.

Weil, Andrew. *Spontaneous Healing.* Knopf, New York: 1995.

Worrall, Ambrose and Olga. *The Gift of Healing: A Personal Story of Spiritual Therapy.* Ariel Press, Columbus, OH: 1985.